# HEYMISCHER HOMEOPATHY

## The Schmendrick's Guide to Remedying Yiddish Kvetches

### Chaim Yankel

475 Hillside Ave.
Suite 5
Needham, MA 02494

www.rightwhalepress.com

Copyright © 2018 Chaim Yankel
All rights reserved.
ISBN: 978 0 9846788-2-2

Library of Congress Control Number: 2017933662

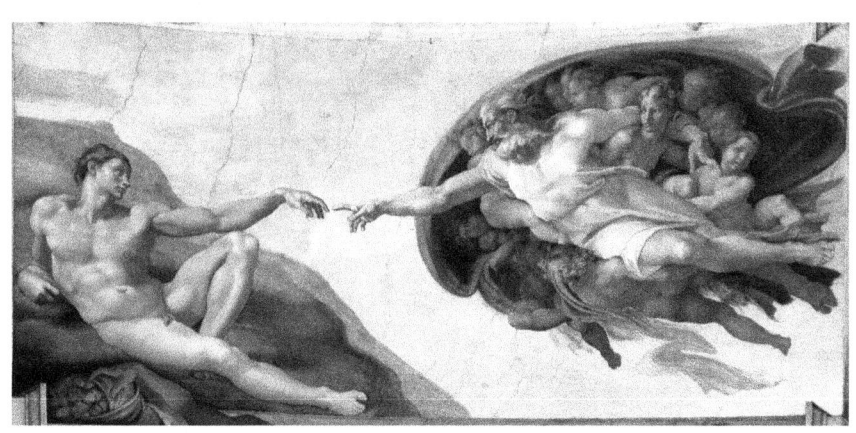

*Got schikt di refueh*
God sends the remedy

*For Scholem Aleichem*

## ACKNOWLEDGMENTS

My gratitude and love to my wife Hannah for her sage editorial advice and support throughout the work on this book. Also many thanks to Doris Yokelson for her invaluable help with the illustrations and to Sima Tsirulnik for assisting with the translations. Finally, a geshrey aoys tsu Michael Wex and Leo Rosten for their raucous celebration of Yiddish humor.

Cover image (cartoonized) is courtesy Quarterlife curiosity
http://quarterlifecuriosity.blogspot.com/2010_02_01_archive.htm

# CONTENTS

## INTRODUCTION

### I. UNDERSTANDING HOMEOPATHY AND KVETCHING ... 1

*Got shikt di refueh far der makeh* ... 1
"God sends the remedy for the disease"

*Der guf iz a shvom, di neshomeh a tehom* ... 7
"The body is a sponge, the soul an abyss"

### II. CLASSIFYING YIDDISH KVETCHES ... 12

## CHAPTER ONE ... 13
*Meshugass*: "Craziness" Kvetches

## CHAPTER TWO
*Farmischt*: "Befuddlement" Kvetches ... 51

## CHAPTER THREE
*Oy, Tsores*: "Uh Oh, Trouble" Kvetches ... 101

## INDEX OF REMEDIES ... 163

## APPENDIX
Finding a Homeopath ... 167

# INTRODUCTION

## I. UNDERSTANDING HOMEOPATHY AND KVETCHING

*Got shikt di refueh far der makeh*
**God sends the remedy for the disease**

In the Old Testament, Exodus 33, the Lord kvetches that the Israelites are a stiff-necked people whom he has half a mind to destroy. Later, when atoning for His grouchiness *Got shikt di refueh far der makeh* (God sends the remedy for the disease). Actually, He sends two (see the **Sheygets necked** entry in Chapter Three).

The first remedy treats tension not just of the neck, but of the entire body. A **nebbish** (poor soul) who qualifies for this particular remedy may even have visions of death.

Foreseeing future need, the Lord sends a second and less dire remedy. Along with stiffness of the neck, the second medicine addresses a certain restlessness: "Gangway, gotta hustle my *toches* (posterior) into exile." Spoiler alert: the remedy is made from the poison ivy botanical, which also cures itching as in: "Oy, am I itching to get the hell out of here!"

### We Are All Kvetchers

An equal-opportunity pastime, kvetching makes us human. More than just complaining, kvetching's domain extends to lamenting, griping, cursing, noisily grieving or woefully wondering.

A persistent kvetch, one that you cannot let go of, issues from the soul. It cries, "My dignity is undercut!" "My confidence is undermined!" or, "Oy, my personality has been warped!" A kvetch that says it all is "I am going **meshugeh** (crazy)!"

We should consider these gripes to be the tip of the iceberg of kvetches, icebergs below whose waterline *rizik* (gargantuan) existential lamentations lie in a solidly frozen state. Heymischer Homeopathy focuses on and introduces homeopathic remedies for these frozen-in-place gripes.

## Kvetching and Chronic Illness

Over time, a frozen-in-place gripe proves ruinous to health. We can say that it *constitutes* the reason for an underlying chronic illness. Since undoing an entrenched gripe offers the most promising route to a cure, homeopathy directed to such ends is known as *constitutional* care.

## Why Yiddish Kvetches?

Yiddish kvetches are poignant. Yiddish metaphors are colorful. The Yiddish language evinces a **heymisch** (earthy, authentic and down-home) feeling. The English language craves the Yiddish touch.

Let's compare English and Yiddish words beginning with "sh." So many English "sh" words are harsh. They convey limitation (shackle, shear, shush, shutter, shy); danger (shank, shark, sheer); discard (shuck); explosiveness (shout, shatter); suppression (shut, shut up); dishonor (shirk); smallness (shack, shrimp, shrink); falseness (sham, shinola); fear, shame and filth (shriek, shame, shit).

Yiddish "sh" words tell a different story. Shlep, shlemiel, shmatta, shmeggege, shmendrick, shnorrer, shpinkle, and shtup are endearing. What's more, they tickle our funny bone. This comic contrast calls for infiltration into the English language.

The quirkiness of Yiddish renders it famously resistant to translation (does "carry" or "pull" convey the poignancy of "shlep?") In similar fashion, a homeopathic "remedy-picture" resists summarization of its core essence in any number of words. Yet, homeopathy stakes its effectiveness on a precise correlation of a core kvetch and a "remedy-picture."

The advantage of Yiddish for homeopathy's match lies in its expressiveness, especially with regard to kvetches that provide indelible remedy signposts. Yiddishizing homeopathy makes it easier to understand and also more fun to study or to teach.

### Homeopathic Law of Similars

The principle underlying homeopathic practice is known as the Law of Similars: "Use like to cure like." It can be summarized as follows:

**"In the appropriate situation, symptoms of illness or disease are effectively addressed by administering a substance whose normal toxic effect induces equivalent symptoms."**

Here, for example, is a usual application of this principle: To keep fear of horseback riding from becoming engrained, one is often advised, "Get back on the horse that threw you." In homeopathy, however, one gets back on a *similar* horse–that is, a horse, but a tamer version of the original, unruly animal. Or, for example, to get over a morning hangover you sip a teaspoon of the same alcoholic beverage you abused the night before. The beverage is *similar*, but not the quantity.

The following story illustrates how experiencing a less painful version of prior **tsores** (trouble) facilitates a healing:

### A Fable

*In terrible misery, farmer Shlomo decided it was time to visit his Rebbe. "Rebbe," he kvetched, "You will not believe what a hell my life has become. My Goldie scolds like a fishwife from noon to night. My five girls bicker and shriek from sun up to sun down. Our frummer neighbor has taken to practicing blowing the shofar at night. And the dog howls when there is no moon. Help me Rebbe! Such a racket, I can get no peace!"*

*The Rebbe stroked his beard. "Have you any chickens?" he asked. "Yes," Shlomo replied. "Bring them into the house," the Rebbe said. Shlomo did as he was advised. A week later he returned to his Rebbe.*

"The strategy did not work Rebbe. The chickens cluck incessantly and what's more, make a terrible mess. Everyone is upset. I still get no peace!"

"Have you a cow?" the Rebbe asked?

"Yes," Shlomo replied. "Bring the cow into the house," the Rebbe advised. Shlomo did as he was asked, only to return to the Rebbe a week later.
"The strategy again failed, Rebbe. The cow moos incessantly and knocks about the kitchen. Goldie is even more upset. I still get no peace. What do you advise?"

"Have you a donkey?" the Rebbe inquired.

"Yes," Shlomo replied, "I have."

"Bring the donkey into the house," the Rebbe advised.

Shlomo did as the Rebbe advised, only to return in another week, kvetching, "Rebbe, this too worked out badly. The donkey incessantly brays and chews on the tablecloth. My girls are beside themselves. I get even less peace than before!"

The Rebbe stroked his beard thoughtfully.

"Ok, here is what you do next," he said. "Go home and remove the chickens, the cow and the donkey from your house." Shlomo complied. In a week's time he returned to his Rebbe.

"Your advice worked wonders Rebbe. I am so grateful. Never have I had such peace in my house!

*I sure hope the Rebbe is right about this!*

The ostensible moral of this tale, "Be content with your lot," is more easily preached than practiced. Why did the teaching take hold in Shlomo's case? How is it that the wretched farmer who first visited the Rebbe was transformed into the well-contented farmer returning four weeks later?

The farmer absorbed something more than a classroom lesson. The aggravation of his core kvetch is what culminated in Shlomo's beneficial rebound. By pushing the hot button of the farmer's suffering with something similar—by cramping his living space even more—the wise Rebbe had invoked the Law of Similars.

Compared with this example, the homeopath–who daily must administer to patients with a chronic illness–is playing for higher and more nuanced stakes; and the patient's experience is not always a stroll in the park. A patient's intense reaction can often result from what is called a homeopathic aggravation. In fact, some combination of temporary worsening of symptoms, intensification of the client's core kvetch, or revisiting of previously encountered, kvetch-related sufferings is to be expected.

The homeopathic aggravation, however, is typically of short duration and bearable. This is because 1) its symptoms, memories, and behaviors are familiar; 2) suffering in excess of what can be borne almost never occurs; and 3) the unpleasantness is outweighed by the beneficial rebound.

It is easily overlooked that homeopathic remedies have an official status. Since 1938 homeopathic medicines prescribed in accordance with the Law of Similars have been categorized by the Food and Drug Administration (FDA) as drugs. This means that they possess greater legitimacy than nutritional supplements, vitamins, or herbs.

## *Der guf iz a shvom, di neshomeh a tehom*
## The body is a sponge, the soul an abyss

The body soaks up pleasures and pains like a sponge, and the soul draws them down into memories and ruminates upon them. A homeopath's aim is to heal the soul as much as (if not more than) the body. The expression *Mit a groissen roifeh gait a groisser malech* ("A great doctor is accompanied by a great angel") thus describes the spirit in which homeopathic medicine is practiced.

In order to succeed, both the doctor and the great angel must decipher a client's below-the-surface quandary, a deep-in-the-soul, existential kvetch broadcasting emotionally charged, but irresolvable issues such as:

- Why do I have **bopkes** (plenty of nothing)?
- How is it that I became an **oysvorf** (an outcast)
- From where did all this **tsores** (trouble) come?

As anguish over these irresolvables increases, inner pressure mounts. Venting via mental, emotional and physical symptoms results, and eventually, we complain of being *krenk* (sick).

Readers interested in remedies associated with a particular kvetch listed are reminded that the list is suggestive, not exhaustive. Also, there are no guarantees! The fact that a remedy is listed does not ensure it will cure the kvetch. To achieve a cure it is best to be treated by a professional homeopath (see the Appendix "Finding a Professional Homeopath").

## Homeopathy's Signpost: The Rubric

Entries within these categories are known as "rubrics." But what are rubrics?

A rubric is the chief tool for fleshing out what a remedy treats. A rubric is an entry in the homeopathic text known as a *Repertory*; the rubric associates a symptom with one or more remedies, each of which is graded according to its prominence within a remedy's sphere of influence.

Like a wide-angle camera lens, large rubrics contain numerous remedies. This lens provides a ballpark view of a kvetch without pointing to any particular section or seat in the park. Its job is to be general. Small rubrics that contain a pared-down number of remedies work like a narrow-focus camera lens that hones in on an unusual, rare, or strange symptom. The small rubric focuses on a specific stadium seat without showing you the surrounding ballpark. This rubric's job is to be specific. In order to narrow the search for the right remedy, a good homeopath alternates between the two camera views.

Wide-angle lens rubrics referencing an overabundance of remedies include: "Fearful," or "Tearful." Narrow-focus lens rubrics offer more pointed guidance by virtue of referencing a subset of the larger category including a smaller number of remedies. Such rubrics would include "Fear of dogs," for example, or "Tears, gushing." An economical combination of general and specific rubrics is essential to a homeopath's winnowing down the number of remedies he or she must choose from.

When encountering a kvetch or rubric that speaks to you, find a homeopath and share your insight. She will transpose your kvetch into standard, non-Yiddish rubrics and commence to ponder your plight.

Winnowing the search for a remedy to a short list of accurate rubrics prepares her for the next key step: Comparing remedy representations depicted in the homeopathic Materia Medica. A homeopath's intake and study of these books culminates in her selecting a remedy that connects the dots between a kvetcher's cry from the soul and his overall symptom complex.

Remedies address psychological symptoms whose relationship to the original kvetch is often not immediately apparent. For example, Natrum Muriaticum, made from sodium chloride, or common table salt, is well known in homeopathy for its ability to release people from "silent grief" (as in, "My husband died and I never shed a tear"). How can table salt help with long-held, unexpressed grief? Hypertensive individuals are urged to avoid salt in their diets because sodium chloride causes fluid to be retained in the vessels with the effect of increasing osmotic pressure. Someone needing Natrum Muriaticum is caught up in a generalized version of this same hypertension, and her *emotions* and *tears* (a fluid reservoir) are similarly constrained. It is this global state of affairs that the dilute version of sodium chloride reverses.

When table salt—or any substance—is put through the special homeopathic manufacturing process known as "dynamization" or "potentization," it develops the ability to heal on mental, emotional, energetic, behavioral, and even spiritual levels. It also prompts resolution of physical ailments that could never be treated with table salt. In the case of Natrum Muriaticum, these include dryness (dry mouth, dry skin) or water retention, as well as thyroid dysfunction.

Homeopaths know which symptoms match each remedy because of homeopathy's method of research. The process, called a "proving," utilizes healthy individuals who regularly self-administer moderately dilute doses of the substance from which a remedy is eventually made. While doing so over weeks or months, they methodically note any and all changes regarding their personal state of being. These observations are collected and become part of what we know about the remedy. As homeopaths use it and share their success stories, their clinical experience rounds out the "picture" of the remedy.

## Homeopathy At Its Most Formidable

Although homeopathy is widely valued for its gentle effectiveness in using like to cure like in acute conditions, constitutional (or alternatively, classical) care is actually homeopathy at its most formidable. Constitutional homeopathy is what my "Yiddishized" presentation of homeopathy is intended to illuminate.

A first-time patient seeking relief from migraine pain might be startled to find his constitutional homeopath inspecting him with wide-angle lens questions. Not only his headaches, but an overview of the full range of his past and present symptoms, behavioral tendencies, life-style behaviors and personality quirks will be compiled. Though of nuisance value to a conventional physician, the peculiar symptoms, behaviors and life experiences of a client constitute a gold mine of clues for a homeopath.

Let's consider a patient kvetching about migraine headaches. Probing the totality of his symptoms, behaviors and quirks lays bare a fertile ground from which the ailment sprouts. Partially hidden within the topsoil of this terrain an existentially charged kvetch is discerned. It might be summarized as:

> "My grief is boundless, but so as to stave off further loss I must do everything correctly. This includes not drawing attention to myself. Though terribly sad, I will not cry, for my tears would be endless and attract unwanted attention. Consolation must also be kept at bay. How am I to honor the depth of my great loss if by doing so I render myself vulnerable to additional loss?"

*I shed no tears so as to deflect attention from myself*

The price she pays for unprocessed grief is the migraine headache. Her homeopath prescribes the remedy just discussed, Natrum Muriaticum. The migraines resolve, but not by dint of symptom suppression. They subside due to her liberation from a delusion that grief release is disrespectful of loss.

## Homeopathy Worldwide

Homeopathy is part of the national health care system in many countries. The World Health Organization **kvells** (expresses warm self-satisfaction) over the fact that homeopathy is the second most widely practiced form of health care in the world. The official standing of homeopathic remedies (according to The Food and Drug Administration) is that they are equivalent to conventional pharmaceuticals. This is why the vials are labeled with New Drug Application (NDA) numbers.

## II. CLASSIFYING YIDDISH KVETCHES

Yiddish kvetsches appear to fall naturally into certain groupings of sentiments or modes. Perhaps somewhat arbitrarily, *Heymischer Homeopathy* has divided a select universe of Yiddish kvetsches into three, broadly defined categories, which are covered in the three chapters that follow. Chapter One covers a grouping of kvetsches loosely related to *Meshugas* or craziness; Chapter Two lists kvetsches arising from *Farmischt* or Befuddlement states; Chapter Three, *Oy, Tsores*, includes kvetsches that spell trouble for the sufferer. Kvetsches within each of these chapters are listed alphabetically.

In true Yiddish fashion, should you find these classifications *verkackte* (screwed up), feel free to dispute them.

# CHAPTER ONE
## Meshugass
### "Craziness" Kvetches

In Yiddish, the noun *meshugass* means craziness. The adjective *meshugeh* means crazy. *Meshugener* applies to a crazy, or inexplicably behaving man; *meshugeneh* to such a woman. Homeopathic remedies can help a wide variety of *meshugeners* and *meshugenehs* plus treat their accompanying symptoms. The following list is a wide net cast over kvetches pertaining to or suggestive of *meshugass*.

# Akshn
Stubborn as a mule
*Far an akshn iz kain refueh nito*
There's no cure for stubbornness

*Silica*
*Gallium Metallicum*

You've already tried the carrot and the stick? So how about now giving the remedy Silica a try? Individuals needing Silica are so detail oriented they cannot see the picture for the pixels. Overwhelmed by the multitude of miniscule details only they notice, it is hard for them to begin. This applies to their bowels too, that tend to move with a stubborn bashfulness. Silica people are intelligent, only slow to get off the dime despite being nudged. Also, terribly self-conscious, not to mention red faced when criticized. On the other hand, they use their anxiety so as to fuel a high level of performance. The remedy overcomes the tendency to being *akshn* by reducing the Silica person's sensitivity to miniscule impediments. A tougher hide he grows.

A more obscure remedy for *akshn* is Gallium Metallicum. The Gallium needing individual is the shoemaker who sticks to his last. His tried and true method of doing things is the best and can never change, as he himself will cheerfully admit.

# Am horets

See also, **Lump**. A *ganef*, villain. The junior version of this sort of person is a jerk, a *shmeggege*

*Anacardium*  *Stramonium*
*Lac Humanum*  *Cobaltum*

The person needing Anacardium is a nihilist (see **Gornicht**) who possesses a mean streak. But this is compensatory since a kvetch of helplessness roosts within her heart. The problem is that early on she has been severely dominated and thus the integration of her personality has been stunted. Perhaps you will forgive her, but also keep your distance.

A Lac Humanum needing person is a *shmeggege* due to being inept in human relationships. The remedy is made from a woman's breast milk (the donor's name is not given). It should be considered for the client who has addictive tendencies, but perhaps also had not been breast-fed as an infant.

With his terrible temper the Stramonium person can appear villainous, an *am horets*. But in this case anger from having witnessed frightful violence can be blamed. So aha, PTSD is what he has. Terror haunts his subconscious. Being annihilated is what he fears.

Someone matching up with Cobaltum is prone to intensely guilty feelings. "It is like I am an *am horets*" he might say, "and everyone knows it!" Objectively, it is not true. The sad fact is that a genuine *am horets* is likely to deny his culpability, his guilt.

# Apikores
## Heretic, skeptic or unbeliever

Within the orthodox community it is feared is that college education will corrupt traditional values, causing a devout *chassid* to become an *apikores*. The word's usage also connotes a heretical, pleasure-seeking ethic such as espoused by the Greek philosopher Epicurus whose name sounds so much like *apikores*.

*Nah, college didn't make me an apikores. I was like that long before*

*Chelidonium*
*Dulcamera*

Chelidonium people are not easily impressed. This reflects their compensating for having earlier been victimized. Stomach and eye problems they may have and cheese they crave.

Eschew discussion with unconvinceable Dulcamara people. This is especially true in the springtime when they are at their worst. It always feels like you are in an argument. Yet for some *verkackte* (cock-eyed) reason the Dulcamara person will deny feeling angry. Forgive him because he may be indirectly kvetching that *zayn mogn iz in a pekl* ("his stomach is in a knot').

# Aroysgebn
To betray. See also, **Moser**

*Drosera*
*Magnesium Carbonicum*
*Magnesium Muriaticum*
*Ruta Graveolens*

Give Drosera for spasmotic conditions, especially if there is a cough and the person fears *aroysgebn*--persecution. This is an excellent remedy for pertussis.

Both Magnesia remedies are for those who cannot tolerate arguments. They must make peace in order to sustain a relationship. They are prone to being betrayed by friends.

Ruta Graveolens treats tendon inflammation and sprain. Lurking in the background of someone susceptible to small joint and tendon ailments is the trauma of *aroysgebn*, betrayal by someone close, a disciple or mentor perhaps. The remedy is made from the herb Rue of Grace and so the expression "I *rue* the day I ever met her" can apply.

# Aroysgevorfen
Thrown out as useless

*Natrum Sulphuricum*

The Natrum Sulphuricum individual is prone to mood swings, depression and dampness sensitivity. If she is in fact not invisible, in all likelihood she has experienced being treated as if her opinions count for nothing.

# Ayngemarint

"Marinated" (like a salad overly dressed). Dressed to the nines. A clotheshorse

*Arsenicum Album*
*Lachesis*


She who matches up with Arsenicum Album is fastidious in dress and will never venture out unless well put together. This is an expression of her perfectionism, a feeling that there is no margin for error.

The child needing Lachesis will enjoy playing dress up. The adult version is *ayngemarint* for seductive purposes. In a snake remedy such as Lachesis the primal instincts (here, to attract and possess the attention of others) break through a veneer of sociability.

# Batlonim
Layabout
*A foiler tut in tsveyen*
A lazy person has to do a task twice

*Sulphur*
*Carbo Vegetabilis*


The Sulphur individual is kind of a mad scientist, an egotist with an active, creative mind but limited follow through on his ideas. A famous rubric featuring Sulphur is "Delusion that her **shmattas** (the duller non-Yiddish books say 'rags') are beautiful things." Discomfort when over heated underlies the many physical complaints from which he suffers. These include circulatory issues, skin eruptions and gastric distress. The remedy will cool him down and make him more socially adept.

The Carbo Vegetabilis person is a *batlonim* because of low energy. Likely she has suffered an illness from which she has never fully recovered. It is a big schlep for her just to get out of bed. The remedy can help cure the mitochondrial disorder from which she may suffer.

# Berye
Top-of-the line housewife. When used sarcastically, a real live wire

*Lachesis*
*Palladium*
*Paris Quadrifolia*

The basic idea here concerns being charming and efficient, but almost to the point of being obnoxious. *Berye* types can include: One version of the individual matching up with Lachesis is a loud, charming, manipulative and jealous woman.

The Palladium person is a diva, someone who needs to be on center stage. She craves approval and is the life to the party. But as soon as the party is over then *nebbish*, she crashes from exhaustion.

Someone matching up with Paris Quadrifolia is a *berye* in terms of being appealing. A prattling and showoffy conversationalist, she is charming until you tell her "Enough already!" Then, surprise! She morphs into a **kholerye** (hellcat).

# Bummerkeh
Floozy

*Sie haut gevain a courva in de momma's bauch*

*Sie haut gevain a courva in de momma's bouch*
She was a whore in her momma's belly

Having found few paying customers there the *bummerkeh* eventually moved to a *shandhois* (whorehouse)

*Fluoric Acidum*
*Hyoscyamus*

Give Fluoric Acidum to the woman (or man) who though lusting for lovers quickly sheds whatever relationship he or she acquires.

Hyoscyamus *bummerkehs* are silly, exhibitionistic and paranoid. This can come from having been oppressed, dominated or abused. The remedy reestablishes stability.

# Chillul hashem
A public profanation, cursing
*A brokh tsu dir!*
A curse on you!

Desecrating the name of God in public usually reflects feuding:

*"You call this gefilte fish? It's way too sweet. I wouldn't feed it to my dog!"*
*"That's a laugh. I have to hold my nose to get anywhere near your gefilte fish, so overspiced it is that you can smell it in the next shtetl I fed it to my dog. Khaloshes* (revulsed) *it made him!"*

*"Insult my gefilte fish, will you? Pimples should grow on your tongue, you Galitzianer!"*

*"Nonstop chozzerai. But what else can you expect from a Litvak!"*
(For more on the Gefilte Fish War and its feuding **mavens** see **Cockamamy**)

*Anacardium*


Though the passionate individuals above may have reason to curse, this is less true of the Anacardium person. Here, *chillum hashem* is a compulsion sparked by scant provocation. When uttering *a brokh tsu dir* it is with hard and cruel intent masking helplessness. In his case, cursing issues from inner conflict and a past history of having been dominated or humiliated. The Anacardium person's anger demands to be vented.

Matching up with this remedy he may suffer a condition known as Tourette's syndrome, a neurological ailment causing people to compulsively make sudden movements or sounds. Known as tics, these can include uncontrollable throat clearing, odd gesturing or the blurting of curse words.

# Dybbuk
Evil possessing spirit

*Mandragora*
*Mancinella*


Not in my house **kineahora!** Having witnessed violence can make someone psychically vulnerable. In Yiddish culture a disembodied being or *dybbuk* can take advantage, establishing tenancy in the mind. Modern medicine would describe the problem differently, as in the diagnosis paranoid schizophrenia. Either way Mandragora, made from mandrake root can resolve the madness and related symptoms that include terror and dizziness.

Someone matching up with Mancinella, made from the spurge plant hippomane can also appear to be possessed. In her case this appears as fear of being taken over by the devil; or fear of her own tormenting thoughts and obsessive behaviors. Mancinella can cure this sort of madness.

# Farbissener
Dour, unlikeable
*Du zalst nisht balagan mit mir*
Don't mess with me

*Don't even think about it!*

*Ammonium Carbonicum*
*Nitric Acidum*

**Feh**. The Ammonium Carbonicum person is bitter at the world but struggles to conceal it. This often results from his having an unloving father or bad experiences with men (if it's a woman). Other features relating to the *farbissiner* state include disinterest in personal hygiene, sensitivity to damp weather, and low vitality. These the remedy will address.

The Nitric Acid person is critical, negative and grudge holding. She does not forget a slight so be nice! Or, give her the remedy and she may in turn forgive you especially if by doing so you also happen to eliminate her canker sores.

# Farshtinkiner
Also, **Paskudnyak.** Someone with ugly opinions, a bigot
*Migulgl zol er vern in a henglayhter, by tog zol er hengen, un bay nakht zol er brenen*
He should be transformed into a chandelier, to hang by day and to burn by night

*Call me farshtinkiner. But you, you're the cause of everything that's going wrong around here!*

*Granitum*
*Nitric Acidum*

The technology transforming a *farshtinker* into a chandelier is not yet available. Therefore we give a remedy.

That might be Granitum, for an arrogant, pugnacious loner. Instability seen in such a personality reflects the fact that the particular kind of Irish granite used in this remedy is radioactive.

Nitric Acidum applies for someone fault finding, pessimistic and grudge holding. The remedy has an affinity for rectal symptoms such as hemorrhoids. This explains why, when encountering a *farshtinkiner* you are tempted to utter the "You are an asshole!" curse. In kindness take a deep breath and say instead, "You have very negative opinions!"

# Fayfer
Braggart

*Veratrum Album*

Needing this remedy is one who is so lost, only he knows the way! His self-righteousness and boasting serve as camouflage. It compensates for his earlier having experienced traumatic, social upheaval of some sort. This may have involved the unwelcome intrusion into his family of a new and appealing sibling. Or, an abusive step-parent has suddenly supplanted his loving father. His experience is akin to eviction from Paradise. Symptoms that betray this unfortunate history include sudden exhaustion, nausea, a state of collapse and numerous mental derangements. These can include a delusion that his portion of food is always smaller than that of a dining companion and many forms of hysteria.

# Gezundheit
Health
*A gezunt ahf dein kop!*
Good health on your head!

Can be said sarcastically, meaning yeah, right, good health to you! On the other hand, if you really are *gezunt*, and never **kalikeh** (sick) then mazel tov! You can dispense with bothering yourself with any of these rubrics.

# Gilgul
Reincarnated
*Ir zolt mer nit visn fun ken tzar*
May you never again experience such pain

*Viscum Album*
*Lac Maternum*
*Bromium*

Viscum Album is called for when medical issues occur because of problems rooted in past life experience. Is such a thing possible? Maybe it is only an "as if" feeling. Better not to argue with a kvetch. Associated symptoms include spinal and rheumatic pain, twitching, and deafness.

Kabbalism suggests that what is thought of as past lives result from the soul not managing to fulfill all the commandments in one descent. The great Kabbalistic sage Isaac Luria, known as The Arizal writes that *Gilgul* requires every soul to cycle (reincarnate) repeatedly until it has fulfilled all 613 *Mitzvot* (prescribed beneficial acts) in thought, speech, and action.

Lac Maternum is needed for when a soul is "insufficiently incarnated." The remedy picture includes ungroundedness and lack of joy in life.

Bromium applies when someone is ready for a new life. Associated symptoms this state reflects or prompts include respiratory problems such as asthma.

# Goldene medine
Fool's paradise

*Sulphur*
*Lipitorium*

A Sulphur needing person can be living in a *goldene medine* if the delusion that "the rags one is wearing are royal garments" (see, **Shmatta***)* applies.

The night following the author's having lead a trituration proving of the cholesterol drug Lipitor (when the pulverized substance is researched by homeopaths) he had a remarkable dream: not only had the beautiful Jewish actress Natalie Portman (seventeen years old in the dream) fallen in love with him, but her parents were enthusiastic about the relationship!

In all modesty, the dream suggests that the drug engenders a fool's paradise, a *goldene medine* notion that forestalling death via its number one sponsor, heart disease confers immortality. The remedy Lipitorium is not yet available. Natalie Portman. Ha! I should live so long!

# Gornicht
Nothing
Nihilism remedies:

*Phytolacca*
*Syphilinum*

Not for lack of a reason, Jews may fall into a black mood. The following ditty, a nihilistic kvetch is adapted from the previously encountered **Bulbes** song by beatnik luminary, Tuli Kupferberg:

*Montik gornisht*
*Dinstik gornisht*
*Mitvokh un donershtik gornisht*
*Fraytik for a novehneh, gornisht pikvelet*
*Shabbos vider gornisht*

Monday nothing
Tuesday nothing
Wednesday and Thursday
nothing
Friday for a change, a little
more nothing
Saturday once more nothing[1]

---

[1] https://The-fugs--nothing-lyrics.

Syphilitic miasm remedies such as Phytolacca and Syphilinum (a nosode, meaning remedy made from an actual disease discharge) are for people with **soides** (secrets). I would like to say paranoia but am struck that Yiddish has no equivalent term. The reason being that among shtetl Jews threatened by Cossack rampages, pogrums, and anti-Semetic edicts, "paranoia" as opposed to being a diagnosable mental aberration was a normal state of mind. Words such as **aroysgebn** (to betray), **fatootsed** (over-the-top-frustrated), **meshugeh** (crazy) or **kholile** (forebodings about the future) verge on what I am getting at.

Subconciously, there is *kolile* concerning the afterlife, suspicion that a vast **gornicht** awaits an individual mired in the syphilitic miasm. This compels him to live for the moment. Though pursuit of material and sexual ends is *meshugeh* his single-minded work ethic can produce inspired results. Physical symptoms include ailments of the genito-urinary and reproductive systems; and problems within epithelial tissue and bones. Overall, the syphilitic miasm state involves tissue destruction.

The Phytolacca syphilitic thinks that life is meaningless. The opposite of someone **edyl** (refined), he is **bulbenik**, indelicate in manner and speech. Because of its affinity for fibrous tissue, the remedy is known to reverse the inflammatory aspects of breast cancer.
The individual matching up with the Syphilinum remedy is secretive, germophobic, and alienated from society.

### Gornicht mavens

Philosophers such as Jean-Paul Sartre need sycotic miasm remedies. See, **Moyshe kapoyr.**

The philosopher was sitting in a cafe when a waitress approached him: "What might you like to drink, Monsieur Sartre?"
Sartre replied, "I'd like a cup of coffee with sugar, but no cream."

The waitress walked off to fill the order and Sartre returned to working. A few minutes later she returned and said, "I'm sorry,

Monsieur Sartre, but cream we don't have-- how about with no milk?"

"You obviously know from *gornicht*," the author of Being and Nothingness smirked. "Coming from me that is a big compliment!"

## Talking gornicht

Homeopathy aids those who are conversation phobic or tightfisted with words:

Harry Korp, a proud and brand new father, sent his parents a telegram: WIFE BORE SON, HARRY. A few days later, he received a stern letter from the elder Karp:

*"For notifying me about this blessed event, I thank you. But a telegram should never contain a single unnecessary word.*

*"For example, why did you have to include your name, 'Harry'? Who else would give a son to your wife—the President of the United States?*

*"And why did you put in 'wife'? Were you afraid maybe I would think Queen Elizabeth made you a baby?*

*"Then you included the word 'bore.' You think I might believe the child was hatched from an egg, like a chicken?*

*"Finally, why do you have to put in 'son'? Does anyone send a telegram to announce the birth of a daughter?"*[2]

Stingy with words is the elder Karp, according to whose *verkackte* logic a blank-page telegram was in order. His attitude is more common than one might think as hundreds of remedies appear within closed-mouthed rubrics such as: "Taciturnity"; "Will not answer": and "Conversation averse." So many that now, I myself am at a loss for words!

---

[2]Spalding, H. D. *Encyclopedia of Jewish Humor*. New York, USA: Jonathan David Publishers; 1969; 291.

# Goyish
Non-Jewishness
No remedy exists for this incurable condition!

*The best recourse may be geshmatt (conversion)*

## Hotzeplotz
Remote, a way out in the sticks location

*Thuja*

Self-isolating from feeling poorly about themselves, Thuja individuals live in a perpetual *hotzeplotz* zone. In the company of others though, they are chameleons so as to camouflage a self-perceived, unbearable persona.

## In shpigel zet itlecher zein besten freind
In the mirror one always sees one's best friend

*Palladium*

The commonest remedy for a narcissist is Palladium. A person needing such a remedy is a diva who needs to bask in the sunshine of approval. Feeling to be constantly on stage where she is expected to shine she is also easily offended, but also worn out from having to remain the center of attention in a social setting.

*Such a punim (cute face) I have*

# Kineahora

When said during blessings indicates one's sincerity. As a kvetch, denotes fear of the evil eye and is akin to "knock on wood"

*Crotalus Cascavella*
*Vipera*

Both of these snake remedies cover fear of the evil eye: Crotalus Cascavella, made from a South American rattlesnake has an affinity for the spectral aspects of death. Someone needing the remedy therefore tends to visualize death in many symbolic, spectral garbs.

Vipera crops up for people experiencing guilt about real or imagined sexual transgressions. They feel the devil will take them over. *Kineahora!*


# Kholile

God forbid! May it not come to pass! Expresses forebodings about the future
*"Death is the terror of the rich and the desire of the poor,"* Joseph Zabara, thirteenth century Hebrew satirist, poet and physician.

*Causticum*
*Digitalis*

Someone matching up with Causticum has an excess of empathy. She is a champion of the underdog and quickly angered by underdog oppressing authorities. Naturally, underdogs have much to worry about for which reason the Causticum person is justified in inwardly saying, *kholile*.

Someone needing Digitalis feels in his heart that something will soon go wrong. Within the chest it is as though his heart may stop beating. Does this symptom reflect or promote the anxiety? Certainly.

# Kholerye
A terribly mean, hellcat of a woman

*Dendroaspis Polyepsis*
*Cenchris*
*Anacardium*

Dendroaspis Polyepsis is made from the venom of the deadly Black Mamba snake. A woman needing this terrifying remedy would be someone who is abusive, insulting, calling everyone a dog, trembling with anger but also likely to wear vivid clothes. Women who have suffered sexual violation may come to be like this.

Another snake remedy, Cenchris may also be considered if the remedy candidate is terribly jealous; thinks she is going crazy; is about to die; and finds time moves too slowly.

Anacardium women are cruel so as to mask an inner sense of helplessness.


# Kibbitzer
One who butts in with unneeded advice. A nuisance, teaser, chit chatter or wise cracker

*Saccharum Officinalis*

Needing Saccharum, such a person (you may recall from **Cockamamy***)* cannot help kibitzing. He is restless, unable to like himself and must always have sugar. Hunger for attention accounts for his compulsion to *kibbitz*.

# Kibosh
To squash an initiative

*Argentum Nitricum*

Someone who is a match for Argentum Nitricum often refuses an entirely reasonable request. So agitated she is while trying to hide her anxiety, a fear that she will be undone by an upcoming ordeal. Then a *kibosh* she puts on the most reasonable suggestion! From her point of view, who knows how many ways something might go wrong? She is like someone within whose head an overly vigilant safety engineer has decided to take up residence.

# Kinah
Envy
*Fun kinah vert sinah*
From envy comes hate

*Apis*
*Lachesis*

Apis is made from ground-up bees. Most honeybees are closely cooperating sisters. They become rivals when a new queen must be chosen. Children with bad sibling rivalry can **plotz** from all the *kinah* they feel! Theirs is an envy obtaining between loving family members, so no need to worry. Apis will fix.

Lachesis-needing individuals experience *kinah* reflecting the primal intensity and possessiveness seen in snake states. Doktor Sigmund Freud, you were right about mankind's need to suppress the instincts. But mostly your insight applies to people needing a snake remedy.

# Kish'm toches
Ass kisser, brown-noser, sycophant
*Honik oifen tsung, gall oifen lung*
Honey on the tongue, gall in the heart

*Lycopodium*

Lycopodium individuals are prone to flattering due to their insecurity. A good idea is to introduce them to Palladium needing people who crave appreciation!

# Khlumus
Dreams
*In khlumus afilu a nar iz klug*
In dreams even a fool is wise

*Cannabis Indica*

An individual needing the remedy Cannabis Indica is likely to have prophetic dreams. But who will take seriously even the wisest of potheads?

*In my dream, behold! The Messiah did not come tomorrow!*

# Knacker
Big shot, cocky bastard

*Platina*

Contemptuous of others, Platina people behave as though they are of royal birth. Good luck getting this *knacker* to take the remedy. Maybe he will agree if he is really *krenk* (ill).

# Kopdreyenish
A head turner. Also, *nachshlepper* is a synonym. Someone who likes a compliment

*Palladium*
*Cicuta Virosa*

Palladium needing individuals relish flattery. If her good looks inspire others to call her *kopdreynish* or a *nachschlepper* such a woman eats it up with a spoon.

Cicuta Virosa people can have excessive veneration for someone. They are the ones who **shlep** their heads *nach*.

# Koved
Honor, glory

Cast your eyes one kvetch backwards and read about **kopdreynish** once more. Can we treat someone *koved* in glory (forgive the pun!)

## Kozak ha-nigal
Aggrieved Cossack, whiny, slapped down bully

*Antimonium Tartaricum*

The child needing this remedy takes everything personally. Very aggrieved is this little *kozak ha-nigal*. She will mutter, go into delirium or stupor. Try to soothe by touching her. You cannot do it without her whining. Also, happens to be a good remedy for a rattling cough with which you can bet, she is also like a *kozakha-nigal* going to whine.

## Kveller
One who has reason to gush with pride and does so. See also, **Naches** and **In shpigel zet itlecher zein besten freind**

*Lycopodium*
*Gadolinium*

The Lycopodium person needs to *kvell* because his insecurity renders him desperate to feel like a winner.

He who matches up with Gadolinium *kvells* because of being supremely smug.

A Platina individual *kvells* because her sense of superiority elevates anything attached to her. By contrast, the Gadolinium person has no choice but to *kvell* due to being so self-satisfied.

# Lump
Pronounced "Loomp," a no-goodnik, scoundrel. Not quite so bad as an **Am horets**

*Nux Vomica*
*Androctonus*


Any remedy type can have a bad day. But wait, the irritable, impatient workaholic Nux Vomica person and the conscienceless Androctonus (scorpion) person stand out. On balance individuals seriously in need of these remedies are likely to be *lumpish* scoundrels.

# Macher

Big wheel, big time operator, someone extravagant. See also, **Knacker**

*Lachesis*
*Veratrum Album*

*Mister Big Shot*

The Lachesis person is a big talker and a manipulator. However! She can also walk the talk and be a big *macher*.

The Veratrum Album person we consider a *macher* by virtue of his being so convinced of his own specialness that others, persuaded that he is indeed special fall under a spell.

# Maven

Expert, really knowledgeable person. When used sarcastically, suggests a "know it all"

*Sulphur*
*Niccolum*
*Adamas*

Mad scientist-type Sulphur people, having all the most up-to-date information qualify for maven status. Of course, they will **hak a chainik** while doing so.

Someone matching up with Niccolum cannot bear to be wrong. Being always right stamps him a *maven*. This is an important remedy for treating someone with cystic fibrosis.[3]

The person needing Adamas has a high intensity ethic about knowledge. Therefore, he is more than likely to know the score.

---

[3]For an explanation why, see Kantor, J. *Interpreting Chronic Illness*; 122-124.

# Mazik
A mischievous person, or a daredevil

*Agaricus*  *Neodimium Fluorica*
*Medorrhinum*  *Tuberculinum*

An Agaricus person is a *mazik* in that he craves stimulation. But when getting it, he becomes frenzied with violent unpredictable movements. Not surprising as the remedy itself is made from the hallucinogenic mushroom Agaricus Muscarius.

Someone needing Medorrhinum is caught in the sycotic (gonorrhea inheritance) miasm. He is impassioned like someone stuck in an orgasm. Does this produce measured behavior? Not very much.

Neodimimium Fluorica people so badly craving independence that they are drawn to violating taboos. *Mazik* is what they are.

People matching up with Tuberculinum are *mazik* out of boredom and thirsting after change. Excitement is what they need.

# Mechiaeh
Self-satisfied, smug

*Fluoric Acid*

A person needing the remedy Fluoric Acid is *mechiaeh* due to his thinking he is entitled to sex with anyone he chooses, or possessing every material object he desires. Not that he necessarily acts on these beliefs. But the feeling he could or should makes him appear smug, *meshiaeh*. If you should meet him, offer a dose to the forty-fifth president of the United States.

# Meshugeh

Crazy (in the narrowest sense). So weird it is amusing. Also, *Mish-Mosh* is a synonym. See also, **Narishkeit**

*Hyoscyamus*
*Alumina*
*Phosphorus*


Remedy states can have both modest and extreme presentations. So someone needing most any remedy can sometimes be a little *meshuge*. Still, a consistently *meshugeneh* woman would be a strong candidate to receive Hyoscyamus. For she is a wild, shameless, silly and even paranoid individual.

The Alumina person's *meshugass* stems from confusion, a feeling like he has two heads. This state reflects his having at an important time in life either been denied a right of choice, or given unpalatable choices.

Someone who matches up with Phosphorus creates a lot of *mish-mosh*, because her boundaries are not strong and she is overly impressionable.

## Narishkeit
Craziness

*Hyoscyamus*
*Stramonium*
*Veratrum Album*


This rubric we reserve for the most overt, out of control type of *meshugass*. Raving craziness.

Veratrum Album is called for when he is a self-righteous religious fanatic. This remedy has been discussed elsewhere; extensively within **Frum.**

Stramonium is needed for a violent and scary kind of *narishkeit*.

Hyoscyamus is called for when the *narishkeit* is exhibitionistic.


## Paskudnyak
A nasty or contemptible person. See, **Farshtinkiner**

# Rugze
Rage
*Der tsoren iz in hartsen a doren*
Anger is like a thorn in the heart

*Stramonium*
*Ammonium Carbonicum*
*Nitric Acidum*


Stramonium must immediately be considered for people with Post Traumatic Stress Disorder (PTSD) as their *rugze* is a survival mechanism rooted in their having experienced terror.

The Ammonium Carbonicum person is at odds with the world. This likely comes from having been brought up by an insensitive or abusive father. Whichever way he turns, injustice he finds. A legacy of bitterness he has inherited.

The *rugze* Nitric Acidum individual is a grudge holder often from having grown up in a bitter and overly-critical household. Hemorrhoids and mouth sores accompany this mindset.
Each of these remedies stokes a constitutional "do-over" experience during which the traumatic weather of an earlier time is revisited so that under more favorable circumstances, cathartic overthrow of the entrenched state occurs. Afterwards, inner storms of *rugze* subside.

## Shlogen kapores
Scapegoating the chicken or rooster: you wave the fowl over the head of the sinful one so that his transgressions are transmitted to the bird. To gain awareness of, and to expiate guilt. See also, **Oysvorf**

*Lac Caninum*                *Lilium Tigranum*
*Cobaltum*                   *Cyclamen*
*Kali Bromatum*

You had a bad day at work? Now come home and kick the dog. The remedy Lac Caninum, made from dog's milk is for people who, like this scapegoat dog feel it is they, themselves who are to blame. Subconsciously, victimization as a form of attention is likely what they are seeking.

Have you heard about those 2.7 million Chevy cars that in 2015 had to be recalled? As a homeopath, I could have told you that Cobalt is a **farshtinkiner** name for a car. The word derives from a German word, *Kobold*, meaning "Evil Sprite." The metal was so named by its discoverers who considered it **chozzerai**. The homeopathic remedy made from Cobalt heals individuals who feel like they should be **shlogen kapores** for a sinful and public crime.

We note how only the innocent feels he is a criminal. Genuine criminals (prone to denial and and self-justification) do not. The GM executives probably did not wave a chicken over their heads after news of the company's faulty ignition system could no longer be suppressed. Still, their crime cost them millions of shekels. A candidate for the Cobaltum remedy would have been the famous Czech writer, Frans Kafka.[4]

No amount of *shlogen kapores* eases the guilt of the **nebbish** in need of Kali Bromatum. Such a person, often the product of a **frumer**

---

[4]Kantor, J. *The Toxic Relationship Cure, clearing traumatic damage from a boss, parent, lover or friend with natural, drug-free remedies.* Wellesley Hills, Ma., USA: Right Whale Press; 2013: 75-76.

(religious) background feels he is morally unfit, in fact, singled out by God for punishment. This can show itself in his face via susceptibility to cystic acne. Strong and conflicted feelings about sex smite him, also an anxious compulsion to wring his hands.

Pity the poor woman needing Lilium Tigranum (made from the botanical, Tiger Lily). She is tormented about her salvation and doomed to expiate her sins and those of her family. She cries, curses, tears her hair, endures wild sexual impulses and thinks she is going **meshuge**. Her problem is trying to reconcile opposite sides of her nature that the name of the remedy itself reflects: the "lily" part signifying religiosity on the one hand; and the "tiger" part signifying sexuality on the other.

The woman matching up with Cyclamen suffers from terrors of conscience, that there is an important duty she has neglected. *Tsoredik* (miserable) with weeping and a desire to be alone, her emotional state can work to suppress her menses.

# Shmatta

A rag, plain dress, shoddy merchandise. See also, **Shlak**

*Sulphur*

The Sulphur remedy is used for a famous delusion, that she thinks her *shmatta* is of high quality, in fact a garment fit for a princess.

*So certain is she that her shmatta is a royal garment*

# CHAPTER TWO
## Farmischt
"Befuddlement" Kvetches

In Yiddish, *farmischt* means befuddled. Inhabitants of the fabled town of Chelm (see the Chapter Three illustration) are legendary for their foolish and *farmischt* notions. As homeopathic remedies are routinely used to treat confusion related ailments, the following list of rubrics casts a wide net over kvetches reflecting how someone is or might be considered *farmischt*.

## Alrightnik
Conformist or one who does it by the book

*Thuja*
*Kali Bichromicum*

Someone needing Thuja is an *alrightnik* in that his self-esteem is terrible. As in the famous Groucho Marx joke he prefers not to join a club having such low standards as to accept him as a member! Conformism and chameleon-like behavior camouflages his anguish. *Farmischt* by virtue of an addiction to over-thinking that obstructs access to his genuine self-interest, his existence is inauthentic.

Someone matching up with Kali Bichromicum is a hair splitter to the point of being prone to a delusory sensation that there is a hair on his tongue. He does it all by the book. Family being everything, his world-view is narrow. Still, his due he receives in that he makes a fine civil servant. *Nebbish*, perpetually clogged sinuses are the price he pays.

# Aylenish
Hurried

*Vet moshiakh geboyrn vern mit a tog shpeter*
So the messiah will be born a day later (meaning, what's your rush?)

*Tarentula Hispanica*
*Alumina*
*Sulphuric Acidum*

*Only a day later the messiah is coming? If I rush I can still make it!*

Someone who always rushes you may need a remedy, Tarentula Hispanica made from a spider. Such a person would himself be hurried, but also emotionally erratic to the point of being destructive. Another quality: he is easily stimulated to move when he or she hears music. Like the comic book hero Spiderman he may have some over-the-top talents.

The person needing Alumina hates to be hurried. She may be constipated, have skin issues, numbness and tingling of the extremities too. Her problem originates in having had her will compromised, in other words having on important occasions been denied the right to choose or been presented with undesirable options. Hating to be hurried is an expression of this "hot button."

Sulphuric Acidum people often feel inwardly *aylenish* due to having too much heat in their stomachs. You will find them to be tired and impatient.

## Aynredenish
Something I talked myself into, a delusion
*Redt zich ayn a kreynk*
Go talk yourself into an illness

Most remedy states reflect a subconscious bias that invites one or another emotionally loaded situation and its related symptoms. Homeopaths refer to it as a "core delusion." But the kvetch, "Oy, am I actually sick or is this *aynredenish*?" is real enough.

## Balmaloche
Craftsman, but when used sarcastically describes someone inept at his trade

*Baryta Carbonica*
*Lycopodium*

Baryta Carbonica people are *balmaloche* due to being so self-conscious it slows their mental processes. But also the reverse applies: brain dysfunction can make him self-conscious and mentally slow.

Someone matching up with Lycopodium is *balmaloche* due to being insecure. Constantly comparing themselves with others, his ineptitude becomes a self-fulfilling prophecy.

# Behayme
Unimaginative person, a drudge

*Got any more filing for me?*

*Graphites*

The existential issue for a *behayme* needing Graphites, a carbon derived remedy, is that he is living far below his potential. He could be a diamond (compressed carbon). Dull, oversensitive, indecisive uncomfortable within his own skin, he in fact suffers with dermatological problems, dryness and acne.

## Biln af der levone
To bay at the moon, make an empty threat, saber rattling

There are no remedies for empty threats. I can find neither rubrics for the idea of making empty threats nor an English verb denoting such actions. Language usage shows that threats are never groundless.

Lack of intent does not explain why a threat is a dud, but fear of retribution nullifying the nasty impulse, does. *Biln af der lovone* is passé, appearing so only after provocation to an aggressive act has passed. Given that expressions of hostility are inherently genuine, regarding anyone making threats as an enraged **farshtinkiner** or **farbisiner** (for whom a remedy may be prescribed) is advised.

# Bulbenik
One who suffers from foot-in-mouth disease
*Az di vort iz in moil, iz men a har; az me lozt zi arois, iz men a nar*
While the word is still in your mouth, you are a lord; once you utter it, you are a fool

*Kali Carbonicum*
*Sepia*


The Kali Carbonicum *bulbenik* sees only black and white, never shades of grey. Self-righteous and inflexible he is, for which reason regularly he is called *bulbenic*. From overly damp or dry mucous membranes he suffers as well. For the body's epithelial tissue prefers being slightly moist, not overly damp or overly dry. Within someone needing Kali Carbonicum the mucous membranes (layers of epithelium) emulate his black and white mindset, tending to be either too damp or too dry. They are insensitive to the gray area of pleasantly moist!

**Nebbish**, the Sepia woman (since the state typically befalls the gentler sex) is *bulbenik* from being worn out and disappointed, usually by men. Her sour fury depresses, exhausts and renders her indifferent. Sarcastic and sharp-tongued from having come to regard hope as toxic, she cuts her husband no slack.

# Bulbes
Potatoes
The monotony of potatoes
The scarcity of potatoes

| | |
|---|---|
| *Zuntik bulbes, montik bulbes,* | On Sunday, potatoes, on Monday, potatoes |
| *Dinstik un mitvokh bulbes,* | On Tuesday and Wednesday, potatoes |
| *Donershtik un fraytik bulbes.* | Thursday and Friday, potatoes |
| *Shabes in a novine a bulbe-kigele!* | On Sabbath, a novelty, the potato kugel |
| *Zuntik vayter bulbes!* | On Sunday, potatoes again |

This song has been transliterated into the nihilistic, "Nothing!" song by Tuli Kupferberg. See **Gornicht**

*Alumina*
*Solanum Tuberosum Aegrotans*

The *fartshadet* (muddle-headed) Alumina person has a problem with potatoes in that for him, they constipate. Sometimes he craves potatoes and sometimes is averse. They still constipate.

Due to a fungal potato rot, two and a half million people starved to death or died from destitution related causes in the great Irish potato famine of 1845 through 1847. A remedy made from the potato fungus, *Solanum Tuberosum Aegrotans* illuminates the suffering: for the remedy picture encompasses: quarrelsomeness, irritability, dread of work, hypochondriacal mood and dreams of pools of blood. There is also kvetching that she needs a change of scenery; that she is miserable and that what the future may bring is agonizing possibilities.

Physical symptoms include rectal prolapse; offensive breath and body odors. To read a wonderful book about the remedy and the potato famine itself, see Homeopathy in the Irish Potato Famine, by Francis Treuherz.[5]

# Chaim Yankel
A nobody

*Antimonium Tartaricum*
*Calcarea Silicata*
*Lac Caninum*

The Antimonium Tartaricum *Chaim Yankel* is a nobody from taking everything too personally. Though an attention seeker, he is also touch averse. When sick this contrariness is rewarded with his getting a racking cough.

Someone matching up with Calcarea Silicata person is a defeatist. He is also someone who likes to converse with and obtain council from the dead. Since those who have passed on are not easily held accountable for their poor advice, this is a *farmischt* and defeatist strategy.

The Lac Caninum *Chaim Yankel* is a constant scapegoat, something he subconsciously invites with his provocations. Because the remedy is made from dog's milk we can say that he who needs is like the dog that gets kicked because its owner has endured a bad day at work.

---

[5]Treuherz, F. *Homeopathy in the Irish Potato Famine*. New Delhi, India: B. Jain Publishers; 1995.

# Chazzer

Also, *fresser* (sounds Yiddish but is actually from the German), a glutton. Compare with **Nosher**

*Fun iberessen cholyet men mer vi fun nit deressen*
From overeating one suffers more than from not eating enough
*Er est vi es iz keyn morgn*
He eats like there is no tomorrow

*Psorinum*          *Lac Caninum*
*Anacardium*        *Antimonium Crudum*

Psorinum is a nosode, meaning a medicine derived from the product of a disease (in this case, the scabies vesicle). The remedy treats many conditions, especially of the skin. Psorinum people suffer from having **bopkes**, anxiety that they never have enough. For them it is like having a **meshugener** accountant inside the head, one who obsesses about what is coming in and what is going out. As the ledger never balances, only future **tsores** he foresees. The Psorinum kvetcher overeats from being certain that before long he will starve. He *fresses* "as if there is no tomorrow."

Anacardium is for the client who eats out of a need to quiet the struggle between his good angel and his bad angel. Such a person crams food so as to stuff down feelings of inadequacy. He eats in an **aylenish** (highly rushed) manner and far too much, so as to squelch inner conflict.

Lac Caninum matches up with someone having a canine, meaning voracious appetite. His overeating reflects poor self-esteem and guilt, a sense that he will be punished before he gets a chance to finish his meal.

Antimonium Crudum *chazzers* are excessively sentimental and also have bad skin. Why do they overeat? Perhaps it concerns the effect of the moon that is known to strongly influence their moods.

# Chelm
## Legendary town of stupid and befuddled people
Location, location, location

*Lining up to see Chaim Yankel outside his Chelm office*

*Camphora*
*Bromium*

We can prescribe Camphora for someone having taken loss of his senses. This may have resulted from familial estrangement as in having been left out in the cold or given the cold shoulder by loved ones.

A Bromium needing person can appear befuddled due to a delusion that strange persons are looking over his shoulder. If conjunct with a sense of being haunted by spirits, his state can be understood as resulting from failure to fully incarnate at the time of birth. In the course of "banishing" other worldly presences respiratory ailments are usually cured.

# Cockamamy
Mixed up, confused, should of course consider relocating to **Chelm**

*Saccharum Officinalis*
*Alumina*
*Sulphur*


The Saccharum needing person suffers from what is often labeled attention deficit disorder (ADD). But make no mistake about his being co*ckamamy* since he is unfocused, emotionally needy, with temper tantrums, dry skin and extreme craving for sugar. At the core this is someone who does not love himself. And so sugar (the Saccharum remedy itself being derived from cane sugar) is a surrogate for love. Numerous books have been written about this v*erkackte* situation. Stop reading and give Saccharum instead.

### Have you heard of the Gefilte Fish War?

Some background: Staid and intellectual Lithuanian Jews, perceiving emotional Galicians as *cockamamy* disparaged them with the *Galitzianer* epithet. Galicians in turn, derided their Lithuanian brethren as *Litvaks*. In Hatfield-McCoy fashion Galician and Lithuanian **mavens** feuded over how to prepare gefilte fish. Galicians said it should be sweet, Lithuanians insisted savory. The dispute was bitter.
Even apart from gefilte fish, the cuisine of Galician Jews was notable for its excessive use sugar. *Chassids* from this area were tempermental and devoutly prayerful. Might their affinity for sugar have had anything to do with this?

*Litvak* preference for savory cuisine in turn, reflected or influenced their intellectuality. This suggests that Sulphur (excessive mental activity and craving for savory food) would likely crop up among *Litvaks* as a homeopathic remedy.

He who is a match for Alumina is *cockamamy* in being muddle-headed. And this is because at some time or other she has either been denied the right to choose or been presented only with choices she could not abide. Did I already tell you this in **Aylenish**? Oy, I must need Alumina myself.

# Chutzpa
Audacity in both the good and the bad sense

*Lachesis*
*Opium*

The big mouth and manipulating Lachesis individual we already met in **Berye**.

Opium people have *chutzpa* due to their high tolerance for pain and living in an escapist, drugged-like state. This has resulted from prior experience of having been terrified. Their escapism reveals itself through overly deep sleep and snoring. Heroic or superhuman behavior during a catastrophic event may be attributed to an individual's having entered an Opium state.

## Dreykopf

A trickster so smart it is as if he has three heads to think with. One who befuddles your common sense. See, **Moyshe kapoyr**

*Cannabis Indicus*
*Mercurius*

Have you ever tried to win an argument with a pothead? You go nowhere fast, right? A person needing Cannabis Indicus (made from marijuana) is prone to longwinded theorizing lacking a point of termination. *Dreykopf* that he is don't waste your time arguing. Instead, give the remedy. Bureaucratic *dreykopfs* may beg to differ but Cannabis is homeopathic medicine and with a little **mazel** (luck) official regulators will agree that doing so is kosher.

The Mercurius needing individual is too clever for his own good. Because he is a trickster who will negotiate every point, best to stand clear of such *dreykopfs*. Or else *geshvind* (quick!) send for a homeopath.

## Edyl
Refined (not overly emotional like a *Galitzianer!*)

*Natrum Carbonicum*
*Silica*

The state of being overly refined can provide context for symptoms. Natrum Carbonicum people's refinement and dignity hides a feeling of being an outcast. A key feature, being overly reactive to the sun also reflects the metaphorical truth, "unable to bask in the sunshine of too much attention."

People who match up with Silica are self-conscious, overwhelmed by details and suffering from other complaints too numerous to mention, all of which reflect a lack of grit.

## Farblondzhet
Wandering about lost

*Petrolium*

Someone needing Petrolium loses her way in familiar streets (but is one place so much better than another?) The remedy will improve her sense of direction but also moisten her skin, skin so dry that *farblondzhet* you can get from staring at the many cracks.


## Farklempt
Choked up with emotion

*Ignatia*
*Naja*

A shocking loss or turn of events, one that turns your life upside down can leave you needing Ignatia. This is when your emotions are intense and all over the place. You are *farklempt* with the feeling of a constant lump in your throat. This is when the remedy rights your ship.

A person needing a remedy made from cobra venom, **gevalt** (lordy!) is a martyr, feeling personal responsibility for a bad turn of events. Despite feeling out of his control, and wretchedly emotional, the remedy will render him less *farklempt*.

# Farshikert
High as a kite

*Cannabis Indicus*
*Anhalonium*
*Opium* and other drug derived remedies

If only you had listened to your mother and refrained from fooling with drugs. Maybe now you would not be in your sorry *farshikert* state. On the other hand, your mother too could be "at fault." If she happened to have experienced terror while pregnant with you, or was once a serious pothead herself, that could have predisposed her offspring to being *farshikert*. Symptoms and tendencies can in fact, be passed down from prior generations. The term homeopaths use when referring to such holdover effects is "miasmatic inheritance." Qualified homeopaths are familiar with "miasms" and can effectively prescribe for ingrained "drug states."

A *farshikert* state can indicate a need for Cannabis Indicus if the feeling involves a persistent spaciness and one notices that the individual spins lengthy explanations that lack a culmination.

Anhalonium can be indicated if the feeling is described in terms of rootlessness, or of one's having a vacuous identity.

Someone matching up with Opium is *farshikert* in the sense of lapsing into escapist mode: deep sleep with vivid dreams, audacious behavior and general lack of reactivity, such as insensitivity to pain.
*Nikhter* (sober) it is good to be.

# Fartshadet
Muddle-headed

*Alumina*

I must be *fartshadet!* Didn't I already talk about this in **Cockamamy** and in **Aylenish**?

# Fatootsed
Mightily frustrated and worn out by it

*Lilium Tigranum*　　　　　　　　*Mezerium*
*Lycyopodium*　　　　　　　　　*Secale Cornutum*

*Fatootsed* Lilium Tigranum women cannot reconcile their sexuality and religiousity. They will curse, pull their hair, strike themselves and run about. They are prone to miscarriage but also, **kholile** (misgivings about the future).

A Lycopodium remedy needing child is immature, insecure and easily distracted. When doing homework he wants to prove his capability. But desire to measure up prompts fears that others are quicker or smarter at the assignment. This distracts, causing him to lose focus and execute the work poorly. With each mental exertion his frustration escalates, leaving him *fatootsed*.

The Mezerium needing individual must endure an unendurable situation due to being torn by conflicting loyalties. Or, he may need to kowtow before an abusive relative from whom he stands to inherit. As if out of spite, this relative refuses to die! Stewing in his toxic juices he is *fatootsed!* Dry and hot his skin will become, and flake off in big patches. For someone suffering through chemotherapy (two loyalties, one to health, the other to the toxic medicines, so literally must stew in his juices) low potencies of Mezerium should be considered.

Matching up with Secale Cornutum she is *fatootsed* in the extreme. She may tear at her genitals, scratching inside the vagina until it bleeds. Modesty is entirely lost and terrible fear possesses her.
By way of explanation: The remedy is made from a dilution of the parasitic Claviceps purpurea fungus found on grains such as rye and barley. **Kineahora**, should one eat bread made from the contaminated grain a disease known as ergotism causing frantic dancing, immodest scratching and other **meshugeh** behavior results. **Tsores** such as befell the Puritan women of Salem, Massachusetts, hanged because it seemed they were witches can result.

Ergot alkaloids constrict the smooth-muscle fibers and the walls of the small blood vessels. They are also psychoactive. One of these alkaloids, tetracyclic alkaloid, lysergic acid, is a source of the famous mind- expanding drug, lysergic acid diethylamide, or LSD. Ancient Greeks required Eleusian temple initiates to swallow a water extract of fermented barley in order to bring them into LSD-like mystical states.

If *fatootsed* and needing Secale Cornutum nowadays, the problem is more likely to concern celiac disease or schizophrenia[6] than ergotism.

# Feygele
Fey, affected, ultra-feminine

*Lachesis*
*Veratrum Album*


Not that there's anything wrong with being effeminate!
Persons who need Lachesis are talkative. If male and effeminate it is in a straightforward, unembarrassed way.

The effeminate Veratrum Album person will be self-righteous and also something of a dandy, meaning possessed of an affected persona. Not to judge but both this remedy strategies arise in the service of a subconscious need.

---

[6]Kantor, J. *Interpreting Chronic Illness, the Convergence of Traditional Chinese Medicine, Homeopathy and Biomedicine.* Wellesley Hills, MA, USA: Right Whale Press; 2011: 43-46.

# Frumer
Pious individual. Can be used sarcastically to describe a hypocrite
*Vos greser di bord, alts greser der ganef*
The bigger the beard the bigger the thief

*The bigger the beard, the bigger the crook*

*Veratrum Album*
*Stramonium*
*Aurum*

People needing either Stramonium or the Veratrum Album remedy are *frum*, but this is by way of compensation for having experienced emotional trauma.

As a result of having at some time in his life had the rug pulled out from under him, the *frumer* needing Veratrum Album seeks (and thinks he has attained) religious infallibility. The self-righteous individual is "so lost, only he knows the way!" A famous Veratrum Album rubric points to loss of social position as the remedy state's trigger.

The Stramonium needing individual buries his nose in torah or bible study because he needs to be saved, from the excess of aggression he has witnessed.

Someone who matches up with Aurum is *frum* but also sincere, holding high responsibility and being genuinely spiritual within his or her religious practice. But carrying so much within oneself is not always good for the heart. The remedy lightens his personality and the burden that he **shleps**.

# Galus
Or, **Oysvorf** (outcast). State of exile or alienation

*Bothrops*
*Elaps*
*Tuberculinum*


Snake remedy-needing individuals are intense. The Bothrops person, having been exiled within his own family is at risk of a pulmonary embolism.

When Elaps is called for, it is usually for the black sheep member of the family, one who is also prone to hemorrhage and diarrhea.

The non-snake remedy of this group, Tuberculinum applies when there exists a need to travel extensively, as the remedy is associated with a yearning to escape. The miasmatically ingrained tubercular condition features respiratory fragility.

# Get
Divorce

*The melamud (teacher) brought his problem to the rabbi. "This is embarrassing Rabbi, but of late I am noticing, there are so many beautiful fish in the sea, perhaps I am becoming a yentzer (philanderer) because I want to divorce my wife."*

*"Now see here," the Rabbi scolded, "that is no way for a Godly man to talk. You, of all people! Surely you know what the Talmud says: 'When a man divorceth his wife not only the angels but the very stones weepeth!'*

*"Yes, I know the saying very well, but if the angels and the stones must weepeth, that is their business. I want to singeth a song of joyeth!"*[7]

*Fluoric Acidum*

You will want to prescribe this remedy for an oggler, such as this *melamud*; or when suddenly a certitude befalls that his or her relationship is doomed. Fluoric Acidum squelches the tendency towards sexual ogling and relationship superficiality.

Not always so easy to get a *get*. A **vayb** (wife) may get **fatootsed** and have to hire a **shtarker** *rebbe* (strong-arm rabbi) to make her **farbisinner** (mean) husband an offer he cannot refuse. In this case the offer can include his taking Fluoric Acidum.

---

[7]Adapted from Spalding, H. D. *Encyclopedia of Jewish Humor*. New York, USA: Jonathan David Publishers; 1969; 153.

# Hak a chainik
## Go on, rattling like a teakettle

A polite way of telling a talkative, garrulous person to shut up already. A similarly colorful expression is *Strashen net de genz,* ("Do not disturb the geese)" meaning you are making too much noise; but also don't threaten me.

*Cimicifuga*
*Lachesis and other snake remedies*
*Lac Caninum*

Cimicifuga people are talkative from depression having to do with being unable to free themselves from entrapment in the needs of a family member or two. A major medicine for post-partum depression, the remedy state features a gloomy sense of having a black cloud over one's head.

Someone matching up with Lachesis will *hak a chainik* to vent her intensity in an acceptable manner, Sigmund Freud called this a sublimation. Such people are jealous. But the venting serves as a compensation for grief.

*Go on, chattering like a teakettle!*

Lac Caninum needing people are full of fears and will *hak a chainik* in response to being someone's scapegoat. Often enough though, the scapegoating is choreographed by the subconscious as they have identified with their oppressor. The remedy is made from dog's milk so think of all the reasons one might take out the bad day at the office by kicking the poor family dog.

# Hinerplit
In a stupor, dazed

*Helleborus*

Someone needing this remedy suffers from what homeopaths call sensorial depression: it is as though a veil covers her face, one that causes taste, hearing, smelling, and seeing to function imperfectly. With regard to touch the same is true in that the limbs feel heavy, numb and oversensitive. **Nebbish**, in regard to someone matching up with Helleborus state, the *hinerplit* state can result from disappointed love.

# Kvitcher
Squealer. See also, **Moser**

*Cuprum*  *Hyoscyamus*
*Apis*  *Stramonium*

Do not confuse with *kvetcher*. What to do with a *kvitcher*? First, give him a good *klop am kopf* (knock on the head). If this fails to teach a proper lesson we prescribe:

Cuprum if he kvetches from being a slave to correctness.

Apis if she is *kvitcher* from needing to outdistance a brother or sister. A *kvitcher* needing Hysocyamus squeals out of hysteria that something bad will happen to him if he fails to express himself immediately. The Stramonium person needs this remedy when his *kvitching* is rageful from delusional need to deflect a (likely) nonexistent attack.

# Luftmensch
An airhead, someone with his head in the clouds

*Luna*
*Phosphorus*
*Amniotic Fluid*

*Will someone catch my drift?*

Luna, made from the moon's rays belongs to a class of remedies known as "Imponderables," described below. Individuals needing Luna are confused, have difficulty concentrating, feel detached, disconnected, like they are floating in air.

Someone matching up with Phosphorus is a *luftmensch* in that she is oversensitive to impressions and cannot process these all at once. She seeks overly close connection with people and is drawn to artistry and fanciful notions. Energetic aspects of nature such as thunderstorms prompt either fright or excitement. Her personality allows for periods of spaciness with regard to her ability to concentrate.

Matching up with the remedy made from Amniotic Fluid is a *luftmensch* in search of identity. His quest reveals itself via naivete.

## "Imponderable" Remedies

Within homeopathy "energy" remedies of which Luna is an example, are not so strange as one might think. Known as Imponderables, they were known about and utilized over two hundred years ago. Constantine Hering "proved" (the term for homeopathic research practice) X-ray in 1897. The toxicity of today's lifestyle and health care exposures has necessitated development of Imponderables made from an ever-expanding host of radiation sources. These include television; mobile telephone, magnetic resonance imaging, and Positronium (an electron and its anti-particle, a positron, bound together into an exotic atom). The Imponderable Cignus X-1 will be encountered within Heymischer Homeopathy.

# Meckhule
Finished, at the end of the road

*Bismuth*

A fictional *meckhule* character that would have benefited from this remedy is Herman Melville's Bartleby the Scrivener. At the end of the road in his suddenly obsolete career he refused to leave the office, muttering only "I prefer not to." In other words he adheres to a trusted, past source of support. This remedy comes up frequently for children who in Velcro like fashion cling to their mother or father.

# Megillah

Long, complicated and boring. One who "gives you a *megillah*," is over-explaining something

*Aoykh komplitsirt. A gantse mgilh ikh ton nit viln*
Too complicated. A whole *megillah* I don't want

*Cannabis Indicus*
*Sulphur*

*Megillah*, deriving from the Yiddish *megile*, comes from the Hebrew word mĕgillāh meaning "scroll" or "volume." A popular narration of Esther telling the story of the salvation of the Persian Empire's Jews, it is also long, lasting five scrolls. Hence, the expression "Don't give me a whole *megillah*."

Someone matching up with Cannabis Indicus will in pothead-like fashion, spout a lengthy theoretical explanation that fails to cohere. Or, what he relates may never come to the point.

The self-centered, Sulphur type of individual is most likely to present a tiresome *megillah* when posed a question. You ask him what time it is and he tells you how the watch works.

# Meeskite
So homely she is cute

*Luna*  *Nux Moschata*
*Antimonium Crudum*  *Rhododendrum*
*Natrum Sulphuricum*

May correspond to what Leon Vannier in his book, *Typology in Homoeopathy*[8] refers to as the Luna type: "Face the shape of a hazelnut; receding forehead with arching eyebrows; nose turned up at the tip; large mouth with turned up corners; round, short, fat chin."

Among the remedies suggested for the Luna *meeskite* are: Antimonium Crudum, Natrum Sulphuricum, Nux Moschata and Rhododendrum. In the event of being asked to treat someone who looks like a *meeskite* consider remedies such as these so as to decide the best match.

---

[8]Vannier, L. *Typology in Homoeopathy*. Beaconsfield, Bucks, England: Beaconsfield Publishers, Ltd.; 1992.

# Mishpoche
Family

*Apis*
*Kali Bichromicum*


Though often a blessing rather than a problem, two remedy states stand out for when the *mishpoche* is supremely important to an individual:

Apis is called for where family orientation includes jealousy such as in intense sibling rivalry.

Kali Bichromicum applies for where *mishpoche* attachment reflects general anxiety and a desire to limit the world to the confines of the immediate family. Needing this remedy, she is also a rule-follower who will split hairs so as to decide exactly what prescribed action to take. Such a person will experience anxiety for example, in the course of getting each detail of a family gathering exactly right. As opposed to showing overt emotion, her stress will result in her body's creating an excess of phlegm.

# Moser
Tattletale. See also, **Kvitcher**

*Lac Equinum*
*Ammonium Carbonicum*

*Moser* has its own, separate entry from *kvitcher* because as the story shortly told suggests, being a *moser* can have more dire consequences.

Lac Equinum is made from the milk of a mare. Horses are high strung so the *moser* needing this remedy tattles out of sheer nervousness; she cannot contain herself.

The Ammonium Carbonicum *moser* tattles out of a bitter need to correct an injustice.

What follows is a Yiddish anecdote about (what one prays is) an atypical *moser*:

*Mordecai, the moser was the most hated man in his small Russian community. Let it be said here that all such mosrim were paid tattlers who supplied information about their fellow Jews to the Czarist authorities. Almost without exception, they despised their own Jewishness even more than they hated their co-religionists.*

*One day when the Russian police felt Mordecai's information was too sparse for the month, he was unmercifully flogged as a reminder that he should be more energetic with his tale-bearing.*

*After the bloody whipping, the rabbi noticed that Mordecai was chuckling to himself.*

*"What in heaven's name can you find to laugh about?" asked the holy man who had witnessed the beating.*

*"It makes me feel good to know that a Jew has been flogged."*

*"If you derived so much satisfaction from it, then why were you screaming while you were being whipped?"*
*"Because,"* retorted Mordecai, *"I hate to see a Jew having so much satisfaction!"*[9]

Mordecai of this story desperately needs Thjua since the remedy:

- Addresses a self-hating example of **Ver es toig nit far zikh, toig nit far yenem** ("He who is not good to himself is not good to another") that the remedy overturns.
- Can subdue his mental gymnastics by reducing his reliance on **moyshe kapoyre** logic.
- Has an affinity for self-deprecation and bitter humor.
- Will kindle access to his self-interest (meaning, his behavior will become more authentic).

# Moykhl
I (do not) forgive you

*Nitric Acidum*

When used in the ironic sense, meaning, "Forget it, I cannot forgive you" that would be reflected by the grudge holding Nitric Acidum remedy state. The remedy softens his grudge holding heart.

---

[9]Spalding, H. D. *Encyclopedia of Jewish Humor*. New York, USA: Jonathan David Publishers; 1969; 65.

# Moyshe kapoyr
"Moses, backwards" meaning perverse, all balled up

*Ignatia*
*Sepia*
*Thuja*

Someone shocked by a sudden loss can need Ignatia in which case she is prone to misconstrue consolation and so, reacts with perverse anger.

Having learned a lesson that hope is toxic, individuals needing Sepia have become *moyshe kapoyr*. This is evident in their sarcasm and aversion to contradiction.

In **Moser** we met the self-hating, oppressor-identified, Mordechai who was so much in need of Thuja. Disabled with regard to accessing his self-interest Mordechai's behavior displays a perversion of natural instincts. His indulgence in mental gymnastics signifies prior history of deprecation. This is in keeping with the sycotic miasm wherein distortion of personal identity and *moyshe kapoyre* thinking are paramount.

Not only the individual, a traumatized society, as well can lose its bearings and require Thuja. Free thinking, argumentative and sensuous France was occupied by humorless, goose-stopping, German soldiers during World War II. This was insulting to French honor and castrating to French identity. Jean Paul Sartre responded with an imprenetrable, seven hundred-page text, *Being and Nothingness* whose *moyshe kapoyre* argument that man is free runs perfectly counter to an opposite lesson French citizens, compelled to squirm under the Nazi boot had absorbed.

Sartre's existentialist depiction of social behavior as "inauthentic" and expressive of bad faith is itself inauthentic, since the term "bad faith" is but a *moyshe kapoyre* term for dishonesty. Insofar as it serves only to camouflage a shattered national identity Sartre's **dreykopf, gornicht** ideology should be taken with a large grain of salt. The same can be said for "situational" ethics pandered by existentialism to deflect attention from the country's humiliating Nazi collaboration. A generation later, *moyshe kapoyre* existentialist reasoning came to infect literary criticism in the *dreykopf* Deconstructionist theory of Jacques Derrida.

Fraught with conformism, fear, racism and hypocrisy, after World War II American society might have benefited from Thuja's being dumped in its drinking water. Here, the identity shattering impetus was not Nazi occupation but shock. Following glorious victory in the war to end all wars, and within the paradise of a booming economy a monster had unexpectedly intruded, a new enemy capable of massive destruction. This was the Soviet Union with its thermonuclear arsenal.

Synchronically, the iconic image of the era's fear, the mushroom shaped cloud of a nuclear blast finds its reflection in a keynote symptom addressed by the sycotic Thuja remedy: mushroom shaped warts. Amidst the sycosis (prevalence of the sycotic miasm) of the 1950's there emerged a *moyshe kapoyre* genius, the military strategist Herman Kahn of the Hudson Institute think tank. His book, *On Thermonuclear War*, envisioned a "Doomsday Machine" scenario while blithely assuring readers that nuclear war was "survivable." Sufficient fallout shelters needed to be dug, so that those emerging from underground could live comfortably amidst radioactive environs and the neighboring corpses of millions. Logical but dispassionate, Kahn's equanimity in the face of (otherwise, unimaginable) disaster is emotionally deficient and inauthentic.

## Mutshen
Nagging

*Kali Carbonicum*
*Nux Vomica*


The Kali Carbonicum needing person nags from a compulsion to make others see things his way.

The Nux Vomica type of person nags from having to be in super control and have things done his way only.


## Naches
Pride

*Platina*


Okay to be proud, provided you are also, deserving. But for one who is "full of it" to the point of arrogance then **feh**, maybe give Platina.


## Narr
Buffoon

*Baryta Carbonica*


The Baryta Carbonic person detests being mocked. So he preempts the mockery, playing the buffoon before anyone else has the opportunity to make fun of him.

# Nebbish

"Aw, poor soul," as a descriptor. When used as a noun, someone pitiable

*Psorinum*
*Germanium*

The Psorinum *nebbish* always worries he has not enough for tomorrow.

The Germanium needing *nebbish* lacks motivation. For him it is enough just to go through the motions.

# Nechtiger tog

Yeah, right, tomorrow! Forget it! That'll be the day! Come-upance retort to an unreliable person

*Ignatia*
*Asafoetida*

Who besides the postman can be depended upon? The question is rhetorical. Yet, two remedies can elevate a person's reliability: Ignatia is for he or she who is undependable because grief has left him or her **farklempt** and self-defeating.

Asafoetida is a remedy that matches up with someone fickle and unsteady due to his being oversensitive and a hypochondriac.

# Nefesh
Naïve. An innocent

*Lithium Carbonicum*
*Amniotic Fluid*


We can say of the Lithium Carbonicum type of person, here is a true *nefesh*. He was "born yesterday," so naïve is he.

Someone matching up with a remedy made from amniotic fluid is *nefesh* in the sense being pure, trusting, and in search of his purpose. Possibly, the question, "What is my purpose? My destiny?" is asked by each of us prior to birth, while floating in the waters of the womb.

# Oy, ikh bin an alter shkrab
I'm a worn out old shoe. *Oysgematert* is a synonym

*Sepia*
*Helonias*

The Sepia woman (for it is usually a woman who needs the remedy) feels like an *alter shkrab*. Too often disappointed, she has begun to find hope itself, toxic. The realization builds within her subconscious that rather than deserving romantic attention it has become her lot to work like an undeserving slave. Her confused sense of self renders her emotionally flat, but also likely to misspeak, transliterating syllables.

*Oy, I'm a worn-out old shoe*

In the Helonias state, there is a feeling of weakness, particularly, a sensation of dragging in the sacrum and pelvis. Also, languor and prostration are found. This is a good remedy for such a woman who also happens to be complaining of an aching back.

## Oy, kreplach

Fear of triangular noodle dish filled with chopped meat or cheese and served with soup. See also, **Khaloshes**

The famous existential *kreplach* joke:

A boy had a fit of terror when he saw *kreplach*. His mother consulted a psychologist, who advised her to assemble the *kreplach* with the boy at the table, so he could see there was nothing to fear. This the mother dutifully did.

"See," she said, "I make dough, roll it out and cut it into triangles." The kid nodded. "And see," she continued, "I take some chopped meat and put some on each piece of dough. Ok?"

Again the kid nodded. "And now I fold over one corner. Then I fold over the other corner. And then, for a the third time, I do the same thing."

*"Oy! Kreplach!"* the boy screamed.

In order to get the laugh maybe you had to be there. The point seems to be that the whole is more (frightening, at least for Jews) than the sum of the parts. Here are some remedies addressing less specific food issues.

| | |
|---|---|
| *Anacardium* | *Hyoscyamus* |
| *Rhus Tox* | *Magnesium Carbonicum* |

The Anacardium needing person can be food avoidant as part of feeling deeply split between helplessness on the one hand, and a cruel need to control on the other. When feeling helpless a plate of food will daunt him.

Someone in a Rhus Tox state is caught up in a rigid way of thinking that converts mere suspicion into the idea that his food is poisoned. From paranoia, the **meshugeneh** Hyoscyamus woman can suspect poisoning is at hand.

If the person is a peacemaker in fear of losing a key relationship the remedy Magnesium Carbonicum may be needed. From anxiety he seeks only to nibble at his food.

# Oysvorf
Outcast

*Elaps*
*Bothrops*

Someone needing the snake remedy Elaps is usually the black sheep of the family. Here is the price she pays for being in this existential pickle: A tendency to black discharges, but also chronic naso-pharyngeal catarrh, with greenish crusts and a disagreeable odor.

An *oysvorf* in need of the snake remedy Bothrops would feel like he has been exiled from his family. He is at risk to developing **feh**, a putrid, rotting carcass-like odor, but also non-coagulating hemorrhages.

# Rakhmones
Compassion

*Phosphorus*  *Causticum*
*Carcinosin*  *Aethusia Cynapium*

We would not want to cure anyone of having the wonderful quality of compassion. But someone overly prone to *rakhmones* might have genuine problems that a remedy featuring this quality can address.

People who are a match for Phosphorus have *rakhmones* due to wanting to connect: with people, nature, with energy in general. The downside to this is that their boundaries become porous, prompting a tendency to hemorrhage and anxiety due to over-connection.

Causticum people have *rakhmones* due to their being a champion of the underdog. The remedy picture includes an excess of anxiety and restless movement.

Carcinocin needing individuals are compassionate due to over-adapting to the needs of others. They cannot deny a request.

It is usually a child who needs Aethusia Cynapium. Due to something having gone awry in the emotional bonding with her mother early on, now all her *rakhmones* is for animals whom she understands and loves above all others.

# Shammes

Many meanings: a sexton, but also a private eye, policeman, or functionary as in guardian of protocol

*Ferrum Metallicum*  *Kali Bichromicum*
*Germanium*  *Niccolum*

The Ferrum Metallicum individual is a *shammes* by virtue of being a determined, defensive policeman type. Noise bothers him too, and his shoulders are usually tight (like an American football lineman leading the charge into the opponent's line).

A sad but functionary-type, someone who operates only within the scope of established rules could use Germanium when there is evident a background of grief.

The Kali Bichromicum *shammes* leads a constricted life due to being overly close to his family. His kind makes an excellent bureaucrat.

Like a baseball umpire, a Niccolum individual must always be in the right.

# Shlemiel
## Simpleton, hard-luck guy

*Baryta Carbonica*

There are more kinds of *shlemiels* than there are remedies. But one common type would be the foolishly self-conscious Baryta Carbonica individual. So as to preempt your mocking him he plays the buffoon. Then, you laugh at his antics not at him! As mockery is humiliating, have *rahkmones* and never poke fun at him. The remedy state results from developmental delay. But conversely, if a child has been made to feel profoundly embarrassed, that can *cause* developmental delay. The Baryta Carbonica child is immature, chilly, self-conscious often sporting a swollen belly and enlarged tonsils. He is prone to hide himself. In old age this same remedy can be used to reduce symptoms of dementia—as when someone suddenly behaving in an infantile manner is said to have "entered a second childhood.

*Shlemiel*

# Shlimazl
Born loser, highly unlucky guy

*Baryta Carbonica*
*Bufonis*
*Hyoscyamus*

This term is hard to translate but it is said that the *shlemiel* spills the soup but the *shlimazl* spills it on himself. Baryta Carbonica we have already discussed within **shlemiel** and the same remedy can help this even more hapless, self-conscious *shlimazl*).

Someone matching up with Bufonis is a sexually self-absorbed *shlimazl*. Though his preference may be to hang out in his room to masturbate, he may also have a brilliant side. In the original version of the film, The Nutty Professor, the actor Jerry Lewis depicts a *shlimazl* of this sort (though no masturbation is shown!).

The Hyoscyamus *shlimazl* is silly, exhibitionistic, and full of sexual prattle that can be both endearing and annoying. The remedy picture includes suspicion and paranoia. For an excellent depiction of the Hyocyamus state and its origin, watch the actor Geoffrey Rush portray the brilliant pianist David Helfgott in the film, Shine. Helfgott's retreat into Hyocyamus is a reaction to having been brought up in repressive fashion by a domineering and alienated, Holocaust-survivor father. The real-life David Helfgott can be encountered in the documentary, *Hello, I am David!*

# Shmaltzy
Overly sentimental

*Lycopodium*
*Antimonum Crudum*


Someone who is a match for Lycopodium cries when receiving a Hallmark card, or when thanked. Though tending to be distractable, he does not get **farklempt**.

The light of the moon will make an Antimonium Crudum remedy needing person markedly sentimental. The other keynote of this remedy concerns her love for food and large appetite. At the same time her digestive system is weak.

# Shmendrick
Nincompoop
*Es felt im mebl in dakhkamer*
There's no furniture in his attic

Also:

*Im hatipshut hayta etz, ata hayita chorshat kakal!*
If stupidity was a tree, you would have been a forest!
Once I gave myself a placebo. It made me worse and I could never figure out how to antidote the effect! At once clever and stupid, this is a perfectly *shmendrick* idea.

| | |
|---|---|
| *Agaricus* | *Stramonium* |
| *Bufonis* | *Plumbum* |
| *Baryta Carbonica* | |

The Agaricus needing *shmendrick* has a mind has that has eventually grown dim from excessive stimulation.

The Bufonis *shmendrick* who is like the brilliant but obtuse Jerry Lewis character in the film, The Nutty Professor was already discussed in **Shlimazl.**

Baryta Carbonica needing *shmendrick* who has suffered developmental delay should also by now be familiar. His mind is stymied due to self-consciousness and having been traumatized by mockery.

Someone matching up with Plumbum has diminished intelligence due to lead poisoning. Her mind tends to dullness and her movements have a wooden quality. At the most extreme she ambulates like the mythical, clay **golem.** (The most famous story involves Judah Loew ben Bezalel, the late-16th-century rabbi who mystically animated a mound of clay to defend the Jews of Prague).

Stramonium comes into play when terror has rendered the mind dysfunctional.

# Shnorrer

Moocher, someone who thinks he is entitled to what is yours

*Az me lozt a chazzer aruf afn bank, vil er afn tish*
Give a pig a chair, he'll want to get on the table

*Lyopodium*

Insecurity can make a Lycopodium needing person a cheapskate or a moocher. This is because interactions for him produce winners and losers. In getting more than he gives he "wins" (while managing also to feel he is lesser, a loser!)

*Now that I'm up here, where are the leftovers?*

# Shteyn af hinershe fis
Standing on chicken feet, having a shaky foundation

*Baryta Carbonica*

A **nebbish,** the individual needing Baryta Carbonica is self-conscious, backward and shy. The homeopathic symptom that reflects his *Shteyn af hinershe fis* feeling is a delusion that his legs are cut off and that he is walking on his knees.

# Soides
Secrets
*Faren doktor un faren beder zeinen nito kain soides*
From a doctor and from a bathhouse attendant there are no secrets

| | |
|---|---|
| *Ammonium Carbonicum* | *Lac Equinum* |
| *Hyoscyamus* | *Bovista* |

Someone who cannot help spilling *soides*, give Ammonium Carbonicum. Having to vent bitterness, this she badly needs.

The Hyoscyamus person blabs as a part of his exhibitionism.

Someone needing Lac Equinum reveals *soides* from nervousness at keeping a secret, but then feels guilty immediately after.

The person who is a match for Bovista spills out *soides* from being overly earnest.

# Tchotchkes
Little playthings, or collectibles

*Kali Carbonicum*

Someone who collects and is possessive of her *tchotchkes* may need Kali Carbonicum, the remedy for someone who sees issues in starkly divided terms, everything either black or white. In order to make sure a possession is categorically his and not someone else's (the inflexible mindset) he collects, thus cornering the market on some definite category of *tchotchke*.

# CHAPTER THREE
## Oy Tsores
### "Uh Oh, Trouble" Kvetches

The Yiddish word *tsores* can refer to any kind of trouble, bad luck or misfortune. The following list of rubrics casts a wide net. Kvetches that even indirectly concern *tsores* are caught up. But so are specific physical complaints.

## Ale tseyne aroysfaln
All his teeth fall out
*Ale tseyn zoln bay im aroysfaln, not eyner zol im blaybn oyf tson veytung*
All his teeth should fall out, except one to make him suffer

*Staphysagria*
*Calcarea Fluorica*

Harsh. But if at the last moment we feel **rakhmones** (compassion) and are compelled to improve his dental health, give Staphysagria or Calcarea Fluoricum.

Staphysagria people--usually women—are overly sweet in the sense of being compliant because they fear anger and loss of self-control. Suppressing their indignation they grow vexed, which worsens their **tsores** because the dysfunctional anger they release is indirect. Instead of confronting their tormentor they might throw a dish or slam a door.

This comes from poor self-esteem, or from having early on in life been taught that to show anger is unacceptable. The inner structure, meaning psyche of a Staphysagria person cannot withstand even the slightest challenge.

More can be said in regard to "inner structure." Clues arise and from the bones. For where in the body is the only place that the bones are visible? The answer is in the mouth: the teeth. Teeth are susceptible to decay among excessively "sweet" people in need of this remedy. The situation reflects or is caused by weak inner structure as well as a typically, excessive craving for sugar. The remedy, Staphysagria will enable her to not fear her own anger, speak her mind and develop decay resistant teeth.

Similarly, the Calcarea Fluorica needing person craves protection and financial security, a psychological need extending also to his teeth. The remedy resolves fear of having **bopkes** at the same time that the teeth strengthen by virtue of "security" being imparted to the enamel via enhanced resistance to decay.

# Alter kocker
Old fart

*Carbo Animalis*
*Polonium*

The person who is a match for Carbo Animalis is old before his time. His poor circulation knots and tightens his tissues, makes him sensitive to cold, swells and hardens his glands. He often has some sort of longstanding debilitating disease. But the main reason he is an old fart is betrayed by a nostalgic longing for the past and grumpish avoidance of conversation.

A Polonium needing person is also a kind of *alter kocker* for his outsized commitment to keeping the past alive. Not so coincidentally, the element Polonium is a key ingredient in film preservation. Had the faded silent screen idol Norma Desmond from the classic, Sunset Boulevard been given this remedy she might have stopped replaying her old films, forsaken her dusty mansion and taken an occasional yoga class. A different film altogether, *Sunrise* Boulevard would feature a less tragic conclusion, but as opposed to the classic film, been a crashing bore.

# Balebatim
Person of high standing

*Aurum*
*Platina*

The remedy Aurum derived from gold comes immediately to mind. *Mazel tov* that he is a *balebatim*. But successful, hard working and responsible people in need of Aurum tend to develop high blood pressure and also serious depression. They are critical and spiritually oriented individuals. A dose of Aurum lightens them up and improves their health.

Matching up with Platina this *balebatim* subconsciously considers herself to be of royal birth and thus, entitled to behave commandingly. Whether a child or adult, she is arrogant and haughty. A sense of superiority prompts contempt for others she views as her inferior. This state can arise is as compensation for stolen or lost domain. Consider a formerly wealthy aristocrat who due to circumstance has been reduced to poverty. Forced to immigrate to a foreign country, his psyche must recreate a realm over which to once again, hold domain. The Platina related delusion provides that very sense of domain. **Nebbish,** among other problems it also includes hemorrhoids. No matter, give Platina.

# Bobkes
Got plenty of nothing. See also, **Kaptzen**
*Parnosseh iz a refueh tsu alleh krenk*
A good livelihood is a cure for all ills

*This I got a whole lot of. Want some of my bobkes?*

*Psorinum*
*Calcarea Fluorica*

Having *bopkes* is a mindset rather than an objective reality. Homeopathic remedies can render you more content about your circumstances even if you are not actually rich.

Psorinum kvetchers never feel they have enough. This is because they have an "inner ledger" program continuously running in the brain. Compelled to be keeping internal track of whatever money or opportunity is coming in and going out, huge anxiety about the future they feel, and suffer itching and chilliness into the bargain.

Calcarea Fluoricum kvetchers feel to be running in place never making headway. Anxiety overwhelms their inner stability. So nu, they suffer from brittle bones, weak teeth, and indurations (hard growths within a variety of bodily tissues).

# Chazzen
Or, *Shreier*. A wailer

*Chamomilla*

Chamomilla is the frequent remedy for the child who, seconds after screaming for a food item throws it away. Capricious he is. Then, from out of frustration it's the mother's turn to *schrei*.

# Chometzdik
A fishbone stuck in the roof of your mouth

*Hepar Sulphuris*

Actually the *feeling* of a fishbone stuck in the throat is more typically when Hepar Sulphuris is called for. Persons matching up with this remedy can seem like hysterics, vulnerable and overly reactive to the smallest discomfort. But I have seen the remedy eliminate the actual *chometzdik* situation.

## Chozzerai
Something disgusting or junky

*Cina*
*Arum Tryphillum.*

Both of these remedy states manifest in irritability and nose picking. The Cina individual (usually a small child) is excused because he likely has worms.

The Arum Tryphillum child nose-picks due to a tormenting itch deep within the nose.


## Dunem in boykh
Rumbling in the stomach (the medical term is borborygmus)
*Es zol dir dunern in boykh, vestu meyen az s'iz a homon klaper*
Your stomach will rumble so badly, you'll think it was a Purim noisemaker

*Lycocopodium*

It's not Purim any longer, so we give the remedy Lycopodium. People needing this remedy are in constant fear they will be "losers" in social transactions. They need to be in control as compensation for feeling insecure (and when completely in control can enjoy the power). With the GI tract his game is played as well, thinking that with insufficient foodstuff it is a loser, though when overly full, a "winner." Not wanting to be a loser when hungry, the Lycopodium person's stomach expresses its insecurity with *dunem in boykh*.

# Es brent mir afhan harts
I have heartburn

*Nux Vomica*
*Lycopodium*
*Sulphur*

Nux Vomica individuals will kvetch *es brent mir afhan harts* because of recent bad diet, when it is also true that she is an irritable and an **aylenish** sort of person.

Lycopodium is indicated if the person is insecure and also a people pleaser.

Sulphur is called for if he kvetches that he is worse from being hot and is often gassy.

*Oy, the brisket. Too much brisket what I ate!*

# Feh
Exclamation of disgust

*Aurum*  *Pulsatilla*
*Mercurius*  *Sulphur*

Many remedy states can feature this reaction. We will mention only these few. The Aurum *feh* sayer does so because he has such high standards.

The Mercurius person winds up saying *feh* because he always finds ways to get himself into trouble.

From having been led down the garden path by some **farshtinkiner** *sheygetz* (scoundrel) the Pulsatilla individual, who is usually a woman has good reason to say *feh*.

Someone matching up with Suphur is a *feh* sayer because of his intellectual superiority to the many *shlubs* (boobs) he is certain that surround him.

# Fleyshik
Meaty

*Bryonia*

People needing Bryonia tend to have a meaty build. They are physically dried out which causes their musculature to be tough and *fleyshik* The Bryonia person sports an irritable personality, a work first orientation and the modality of feeling better when motionless. The remedy is made from a botanical, namely hops. This is a vine whose determination to climb and cling is mirrored in the Bryonia individual who while clinging to support from those closest to him, is himself upwardly mobile. His *tsores* involves a frustrating quest for financial well-being.


# Fortz
Fart
*Azoy fil ritzinoyl zol er oystrinkn*
He should drink too much castor oil

*Carbo Vegetabilis*
*Lycopodium*

Drinking too much castor oil works both as a punishment and a treatment. But if the client balks, then the remedy Carbo Vegetabilis for someone almost completely exhausted--like the burnt out ember from which the remedy is made--is called for.

Lycopodium, made from a short, sprouting moss, and appropriate for the insecure people pleaser will help to squelch the *fortzing*.

# Fransn
Venereal disease
*Fransn zol esn zayn layb*
Venereal disease should eat his flesh!

*Syphilinum*                *Medorrhinum*
*Mercurius*                 *Thuja*


You say my daughter intends to marry him? **Gevalt!** This changes everything. *Geshvind* (quick!) bring me my remedies! What we face here is a legacy problem: inherited tendencies passed down from *fransn* afflicted ancestors. Whether genetically or epigenetically rooted, homeopaths refer to such vestigial effects as a miasm.

Let God speed my cure with the highest strength Syphilinum or Mercurius. In the event there is a family history of syphilis (the syphilitic miasm) this will be even more urgent since his also, now my own progeny are prone to secrecy, shamefulness, depression, circular thinking and congenital ailments.

If he has a family history of gonorrhea (the sycotic miasm) then my **tsores** will include worrying that his and my own offspring will develop respiratory and skin ailments, identity issues (see **Moyshe kopyre**) and anguish. Blessedly, the remedies Medorrhinum and Thuja are at hand.

## Geshvir
Boil
*A geshvir iz a guteh zach bei yenem untern orem*
A boil is fine as long as it's under someone else's arm

*Hepar Sulphuris*
*Silica*


When the boil happens to be under your own arm the best remedies are: Hepar Sulphuris when the symptomatic context for the *geshvir* features hyper-vulnerability.

Silica for a sensitive, self-conscious individual who possesses an eye for details.


## Gevalt
Yikes! Also, **Oy Gevalt** (Oh no! Misfortune!)

*Aconite*
*Gelsemium*
*Apis*


Aconite is called for in the event of panic from sudden shock. Veratrum Album is for when the shock is from sudden loss of social position.

Gelsemium is for when a person is shaky and frightened following a setback.

Apis is needed following shock such as sudden widowhood, where means of livelihood are undermined and a woman's hormones become disharmonized.

# Gey kocken oiffen yam
Go defecate in the ocean

*Aloe*
*Muriatic Acidum*

Be careful of what you wish for. For example, if this curse is complied with you too may suffer. We now consider the related ailment, involuntary stool. For when poop happens, two helpful remedies we mention:

Aloe, when general loss of tone due to overly sedentary lifestyle is at play.

Muriatic Acidum, for when a *verkackte* relationship with one's mother prompts despair. The **fatootsed** mindset can loosen the bowels.

*Feh. It's nothing to be proud of*

# Glitsch
Slip-up or goof up
Having crossed over into English usage is the idea of a mistake or a goof up. The Yiddish meaning though is literal, a physical slip

*Cuprum*

Cuprum is indicated for when one catches oneself during a slip on ice and in a protective reaction, the muscles suddenly clench and go into a painful spasm.

# Golem
Robot, zombie, having no grace, a simpleton

*Plumbum*

Plumbum is made from lead. Therefore its remedy picture largely represents lead poisoning featuring numbness and stiffness from neurological damage. This can cause unnatural, *golem*-like movements and cognitive delay. For kvetching about having excessive strength like Rabbi Lowe's legendary Prague protector, maybe look at remedies under **Shtarker**. As children are susceptible to mental dulless due to lead poisoning, Plumbum recommends itself as a pediatric remedy.

# Grepser
Belcher

*Argentum Nitricum*

Whoever matches up with Argentum Nitricum belches because of being caught in an anxious certitude that all her endeavors are ordeals. This agitates her stomach. She is also *verkackte* in that her nervousness makes her liable to refuse even the most reasonable request. Also see, **Fortz**.

# Heymisch
Friendly, informal, homey, down home

*Bovista*

The Bovista needing person is so socially uncomfortable and prone to stammering it is impossible to feel insecure in her presence. Blunt and ready to spill secrets explains why she comes across as *heymisch*. Especially when applying to a woman, the remedy state features hormonal imbalance and general puffiness of the skin.

# Kadokhes
Fever and chills

*Hundert hayzer zol er hobn, in yeder hoyz a hundert tsimern, in yeder tsimer tsvonsik betn un kadokhes zol im varfn fin eyn bet in der tsveyter*
A hundred houses shall he have, in every house a hundred rooms and in every room twenty beds, and a delirious fever should drive him from bed to bed

*Arsenicum*
*Gelsemium*
*Natrum Muriaticum*


When calling the homeopath make sure to specify through which of the hundred houses, hundred rooms and twenty beds your kvetcher is feverishly hurtling! When located one of the following remedies is likely to be needed:

Arsenicum is a good choice for fever with restlessness driving one out of bed.

Gelsemium if she has chills, due to an emotional setback.

Natrum Muriaticum is called for if she is feverish and also possessed of a constrained demeanor. An example of this would be being unable to produce tears except when when apart from others.

## Kaken mit blit un mit ayter
Stool mixed with blood and pus
*Er zol kakn mit blit un mit ayter*
He should crap blood and pus

*Thuja*

The sentiment could be nobler but in the event he is soon to be your houseguest, consider giving him Thuja. Yes, we are dealing with a problem rooted in the same poor self-esteem issue discussed in **Moser.**

## Kalikeh
A sickly person
*Zolst helfen vi a toiten bankes*
Trying to help here is like blood-cupping a corpse

*Cina*

A vain kvetch, since the prognosis is poor. But wait. Certain remedies avail. Cina for children with a sickly look, for example. They are *kalikeh* probably from having worms.

# Kaptzen
Despicable pauper

*Hydrocyanicum Acidum*
*Leprominium*

As Michael Wex, author of Born to Kvetch points out, Yiddish is often subversive and politically incorrect. But oy, this unfortunate word. Preferable is the sentiment voiced by Scholem Aleichem's Tevye the Milkman, "Lord, it's no disgrace to be poor, but it's no great honor either!"

*Der dales laigt zikh tsum ershten oifen ponem*
Poverty reveals itself first on the face

*Kaptzen's* existence within language exposes a verity that the poor are often despised, a truth with homeopathic value. Suggested by this word is the leprosy miasm, a condition featuring unremitting struggle attached to a loathsome self-image. Blessedly, a *kaptzen* state of affairs is lifted by a remedy such as Hydrocyanic Acid or the leprosy nosode (a bodily product of the disease itself), Leprominium.


# Kile
Hernia

*Nux Vomica*


Here is a riddle. What is the Asian city named for it's containing so many workaholic individuals? Answer: Taipei (pronounced Type A), forgive the pun. "Nuxers" are Type A, impatient, irritable, forever multi-tasking, and tightly wound. So many such people need Nux Vomica. And are prone to *kile* as well? One shouldn't wonder.

# Khaloshes
Revulsion for food. See also, **Oy, Kreplach!** and **Loksh**
*Ess vie ein foygl sheise vie ein ferd*
Eat like a bird, excrete like a horse

*Antimonium Tartaricum*
*Kali Carbonicum*


The Antimonium Tartaricum needing person can have a scant appetite and takes everything personally. Touchy!

The Kali Carbonicum bird-like eater is judgmental, and intolerant of opinions she regards as wrong. Her mucous membranes are always either dry or damp. Both of these remedy types, once they get it into their mind that food is undesired go overboard with that. *Khaloshes* results.


# Khalutz
Pioneer, as in an idealistic zealot settling a new land. If out of clumsiness you pick the wrong land, a similar sounding but different word applies, **Klutz** (blockhead)

*Tuberculinum*


The lung compression that Tuberculosis causes stokes an inheritable (miasmatic) craving for fresh air, liberty, open spaces and romantic impulse. Desire to travel and pioneer expeditions are the good parts. The remedy thus addresses the flip side of the *khalutz* picture: allergies, food sensitivities and erratic behavior.

# Khmalye
A clout on the head, a *Klop*. Also, read **Lokh in kopf**

*Arnica*
*Natrum Sulphuricum*


Arnica, the first choice in all situations of musculo-skeletal trauma is critically important for concussion. It belongs by the bucketful on all football fields. A key indication involving shock is the injured party's denying anything is wrong. It is as if unhappy with the state of affairs the soul has partially vacated the premises. Arnica "retrieves the soul" thereby energizing the immune system and its healing response.

Use Natrum Sulphuricum after Arnica, for someone who had suffered a head trauma and is still not her usual self. A person deeply in need of this remedy will also be sensitive to mold, and prone to a depressive notion of being perpetually overlooked.

We have already discussed the mean Anacardium needing person who if a woman, can be a *kholerye*.


# Kishkes
Intestines

*Cyclamen*
*Thuja*


Someone who matches up with Cyclamen has pain in the *kishkes* from feeling she has neglected her duty. *Ach*, this is mainly a woman's remedy.

Thuja people suffer in the *kishkes* from leading inauthentic lives. But many other remedies also stop kvetching due to intestinal pain.

# Klutz
Clumsy, awkward, a blockhead, a dolt. See also, **Behayme**

*Apis*
*Capsicum*

The person needing Apis can be *klutzy*. Often, this is because for her, creating or having a family is at odds with the demands of a career. The conflict between creativity and procreativity is overly challenging.

Capsicum needing individuals are stereotypically fat, lazy, lacking in vitality, mentally clouded and often homesick. Also, clumsy.

People matching up with the remedy Staphysagria happen to be prone to a forehead pain that feels *klutzy*, like an enlodged block of wood. Rather than *klutzes*, they are intelligent, over-sensitive people who dread confrontation.

# Kramp
Cramp
*A kramp im in layb*
Bodily cramps

*Cuprum*
*Magnesium Phosphoricum*

Cuprum needing people are emotionally cramped. Also, ambitious and readily angered when others do not follow the rules as the Cuprum person sees them.

People matching up with Magnesium Phosphoricum are always kvetching about their pains. Menstrual pains can, **nebbish**, be severe with terrible *kramp*.

# Krets
Scabies
*Er zol hobn paroys makes bashotn mit oybes krets*
He should have Pharaoh's plagues sprinkled with Job's scabies

*Psorinum*

**Feh.** Pharaoh's plagues require yet a whole other book to discuss. But for *krets* we have the wonderful Psorinum remedy. For when you find she is always also keeping track of what she has or has not, what resources are coming in or flowing out. A crazed accountant and his ledger book have taken up residency in her head.

# Krikh arayn in di beyner
Crawls into my very bones, gets under my skin

*Aurum*
*Culex*
*Formica*

Give Aurum for when the bones aching and the kvetcher is overly responsible.

Culex applies to pacify an annoying gossiper that we can compare with the pesky mosquito from which the remedy is made (see also, **Yente**). Symptoms include intense itching.

Formica should be given if the kvetch includes formication (medical term for the sensation of ants swarming under the skin). Not surprising as the remedy is made from ants!

# Kvetcher

Complainer, griper, one who strains or fusses. A synonym is *burtscher*
*A khasuren di kalleh is tsu shayn*
A fault-finder complains even that the bride is too beautiful

*Angustera Vera*          *Calcarea Phosphoricum*
*Antimonium Tartaricum*   *Nux Vomica*
*Ammonium Carbonicum*     *Zincum*

In Heymisher Homeopathy kvetches encompass gripes, curses and angst. Here we examine the kvetch in its narrower sense.

Angustera Vera matches up with the kvetcher who is extraordinarily tight, to the point where muscular stiffness verges on a paralysis like, muscular lock-down. He is oversensitive, capricious and filled with bitterness. In homeopathic thinking his symptoms are a vestige: miasmatic influence from a legacy of tetanus.

Antimonium Tartaricum is for the whining type of kvetcher.

Ammonia Carbonicum is for the bitching and moaning type of kvetcher.

Nux Vomica is for relief from straining on the toilet. The "Nuxer" is not anywhere near so tight as someone needing Angustera Vera, but still, tense to the point of kvetching. Alas, the more he strains the more tense he becomes.

Calcarea Phosphoricum people kvetch from being undecided about what is more important, safety and stability or being venturesome. Everything gives them cause to kvetch, most of all bad news (not that many of the rest of us enjoy being disappointed). Restlessness, quick to be bored and suffering joint pains, this describes the Calcarea Phosphoricum person. A good remedy to give to your teenager whose personality in the wake of a sudden growth spurt has changed for the worse.

Zincum kvetchers make mountains out of molehills and tend to repeat some or another annoying behavior over and over. Thinking overtires them. Usually a parental issue, having a father who is emotionally distant underlies the problem.

## Laksirekhts
Diarrhea

*A distraught mother came to a chassid (orthodox Jew) about her sick child.*

*"Rebbe," she lamented, "my child is suffering already a whole week from laksirekhts. I tried every medicine, but nothing will stop it!"*

*"Don't worry," the chassidic rabbi comforted her. "All you need to do is say teffilim (chant the texts of the Psalms). I have no doubt you will witness a miracle."*

*Three days later the worried mother reappeared at the rabbi's house. "Rebbe, I did exactly as you suggested, but now my little boy is suffering from the opposite symptoms. He can't go at all!"*

*"Say again teffilim," recommended the chassid.*

*"But rabbi," protested the woman, "teffilim are constipating!"*[10]

Traditional Chinese Medicine theory teaches that whenever the stools are loose the Spleen is disharmonized. The ancient Chinese held that the Spleen organ rules metabolism, meaning the transportation and transformation of fluids. The organ is happiest when dry but grumpiest when damp. Dampness occurs from exposure to weather extremes; or when the Spleen's "host" worries too much. This disharmonizes the Spleen causing stools to loosen and *laksirekhts* to result. As hundreds of remedy states display anxiety and worry. I will mention only a few where cares figure prominently.

---

[10]Adapted from Spalding, H. D. *Encyclopedia of Jewish Humor*. New York, USA: Jonathan David Publishers; 1969; 82.

*China Officinalis*
*Arsenicum Album*
*Podophyllum*

Someone needing China Officinalis develops *laksirekhts* from a sense of persecution. High strung and idealistic, she worries that the world does not conform to her ideals. She grows irritable and dehydrated.

He who matches up with Arsenicum is a perfectionist. His anxiety stems from a subconscious sense that due to time running out, there is scant margin for error in his endeavors or his need to safe-keep those he loves. His body's circulation grows disharmonized, causing hot and cold energies not to communicate. *Laksirekhts* but also constipation can result.

Podophillum I will mention as primarily an acute care remedy. Here, dampness disturbs the Spleen. This is from a climate source, such heat of the summer.

# Lokh in kopf
Hole in the head

*Arnica*
*Natrum Sulphuricum*
*Cygnus X-1* (belonging to a class of remedies known as "Imponderables" introduced in **Luftmensch**)


As we saw in **Kmalye,** Arnica the principal remedy for musculo-skeletal injury is also excellent for head injuries, concussions that one needs like a hole in the head.

After Arnica, it often makes sense to give Natrum Sulphuricum. Conventional medicine has no equivalent.

Professors Einstein and Hawking can *kvell*. Not only has their prediction that galactic black holes exist been confirmed, but a homeopathic has been made from the energy of one such black hole. Are you are curious as to how this miracle came about? The remedy was made by means of a vial of alcohol being affixed to the viewing end of an 8" telescope's aperture (Meade LX90) as the telescope was focused on Cygnus X-1's location within the Cygnus constellation. The remedy Cygnus X-1 comes into play for individuals whose *lokh in kopf* is a sensation feeling like a vortex into which they are being sucked.

# Loksh
Someone skinny as a noodle

*Iodium*
*Calcarea Phosphoricum*

*But maybe a basketballer I can be?*

Iodium would be the chief remedy for such an individual since it is prominent in the rubric "emaciation." People needing this remedy cannot bear silence but also exhibit a desperate obsessiveness.

Calcarea Phosphoricum individuals are loksh due to a metabolic issue. Perhaps their engrained crankiness (they are never pleased) is at fault.

## Makekhs vaksen offen tsung
Tongue ulceration. Medical term is aptha or stomatitis
*Zol makekhs vaksen offen tsung!*
Pimples should grow on his tongue!

*Helleborus*
*Natrum Phosphoricum*
*Nitric Acidum*


Helleborus is given if, in addition to the pimply tongue, it is as though he is not mentally present, for it seems a veil is cloaking his senses.

Natrum Phosphoricum can be given if in addition to having the apthae she is fearful, easily startled from noise, and (sometimes!) upon waking at night thinks her furniture is alive. **Gevalt.**

Nitric Acidum is needed if the person's grudge-holding and bitterness accounts for the outbreak.


## Milkhik
Pale as milk, sickly looking. See also, **Kalikeh**

*Psorinum*
*Cina*
*China Officinalis*


The Psorinum person is *milkhik* from worry that he never has enough.

It is usually a child who matches up with Cina. She is pale from irritation because of having intestinal worms.

The person needing China Officinalis is pale, most often from dehydration.

## Nosher
Snacker. Compare with **Chazzer**

*Lycopodium*
*Saccharum Officinalis*


The Lycopodium person *noshes* because his interactions, including those with food are "political." It's all about power: he won't let food get the better of him.

A Saccharum Officinalis needing person does not loves himself so cannot be satisfied by food. Sweets, a cheap stand-in for love are his downfall.


## Nudne
Boring, but also see **Behayme** and **Bulbes**
*Kreplakh esn vert oykh nimes*
One gets tired of eating only dumplings

*Calcarea Phosphoricum*


For the bored, dissatisfied individual, often one's own *kind* (child) Calcarea Phosphoricum can be a blessing. After taking the remedy he'll say, "Hey! What did you do different? These dumplings taste great!"

# Nudnik

An annoying, trying person. A noodge

*Hepar Sulphuris*
*Tarentula Hispanica*

The Hepar Sulphuris *nudnik* is irritable due to being overly sensitive to physical stimuli. For example, a child who becomes hysterical when going outside in wintertime a bit of ice gets into his sleeve.

Someone needing the spider remedy Tarentula Hispanica is a *nudnik* from tremendous inner need to jump around especially when hearing music. This can be to the point of destructiveness.

# Ongepatshket

Sloppy, messed up. See also **Shmatta**
*Besser a miesseh lateh aider a shaineh loch*
Better to have an ugly patch than a beautiful hole

*Sulphur*

His clothes can be full of holes or ugly patches. It makes little difference. At his most extreme, the slovenly, mad scientist type of Sulphur individual will neglect even to bathe.

# Oy! Es falt fun di hent
Yikes! I keep dropping things

*Apis*  *Bovista*
*Moschus*  *Nux Vomica*

The Apis person is clumsy because of the agitation produced by an internal tension: need to physically reproduce that is opposed by desire to be productive in work. The remedy, made from crushed angry bees reflects the industriness of bees and a violent, reproduction related drama that attends selection of a new queen. Sibling rivalry afflicting the person needing Apis is mirrored by the hive's social dynamics, themselves ruled by competition among a multitude of sister bees.

Someone matching the description of Bovista is clumsy due to general awkwardness, excessive sincerity and taking amiss, inoffensive remarks.

An individual needing Moschus drops things because he is so readily frightened. He is like a deer caught in the headlights.

A Nux Vomica person drops things out of impatience as he is too keen on getting through one activity and moving on to the next.

# Oysmus
Scolding

*Marrying a shiksa? This we needed!*

| | |
|---|---|
| *Chelidonium* | *Lycopodium* |
| *Stramonium* | *Moschus* |

The Cheldonium needing person is prone to *oysmus* from disdain of authoritarian behavior.

If she scolds because she feels less like a loser if her control is threatened, give her Lycopodium.

Someone matching up with Moschus scolds until she is blue in the face. But this is because she is almost **fatootsed.**

Someone in need of Stramonium is prone to *oymus* to vent terror of annihilation.

# Patshke
To mess around, engage in fruitless activity. Someone with **Shpilkes**

*Aranea Diadema*

Made from a spider is this remedy, Aranea Diadema. People needing it are prone to fidgeting and every kind of *patshkying* around. In addition they are oversensitive to dampness and susceptible to sensations of numbness and imagining enlargement of body parts.

# Petseleh
Small penis

*Agnus Castus*
*Selenium*

Of course, for one with a genuine *petseleh,* other than to recommend a crash course in lovemaking skills little can be done. If the problem is *hinken shmok* (limp penis), Agnus Castus comes in handy. Consider the remedy when the limpness is adjoined to poor memory, self-contempt and fear of death.

Let's say the client kvetches of dribbling semen during sleep, loss of sexual power; or that his *petsel* relaxes as soon **shtupping** (intercourse) starts. Telling this to his acupuncturist, he may hear from her, just before she reaches for her needles and begins gathering up herbs, "Oy, Kidney deficiency!" The homeopathic remedy Selenium fits this Traditional Chinese diagnosis in many respects. But for something to make an erection stronger than normal, don't ask! If I knew that, then rich like the Viagra **mavens** I would be!

# Pisher
Neophyte, or for kvetch purposes, a bed wetter

*Causticum*
*Mandragora*
*Equisetum*

The Causticum individual, generally a child, is a *pisher* from anxiety. Such children are sincere and open. But when disappointed it is as if they suddenly scrunch themselves up, after which they must slowly open again like a flower. This "open and close" dynamic is actually the structure of a spasm, whose energy suffuses the child's being. The bladder, being characterized by contraction and release is overly reactive in the heightened Causticum state. Thus, a child is likely to wet the bed. Giving birth can cause a full-grown woman to develop a *pishing* problem too. She may lose urine from coughing, laughing or sneezing. Causticum as well as a sense of humor keeps her from kvetching about it.

A Mandragora individual has the *pishing* problem due to having been frightened by a violent event he has witnessed.

Equisetum is commonly used for this condition (that also goes by the name of enuresis) but the remedy's mental and emotional theme is hard to pin down.

# Plotz
To burst, explode

*Kali Carbonicum*  *Lycopodium*
*Carbo Vegeatabilis*  *Lachesis*
*Bovista*


Kali Carbonicum is a remedy for the intolerant individual whose anxiety at encountering injudicious opinions causes such stomach anxiety he could *plotz*.

A person needing Lycopodium could *plotz* after a meal because he eats too much out of insecurity.

Carbo Vegetabilis people have a stagnant digestive system. It feels as if nothing seems to move within the abdomen. This is why they too, could *plotz* after eating.

People matching up with Lachesis and Bovista will not *plotz* due to eating. But their sensitivity to abdominal pressure or anything tight around the waist can make them feel that way.

*I could plotz from all the latkes I ate*

# Sheygets necked
Stiff necked

*Crotalus Cascavella*
*Rhus Tox*

In Exodus 33 the Lord kvetches that the Israelites are a stiff-necked people whom he has half a mind to destroy. Later, in a better mood, *Got shikt di refueh far der makeh*, God sends the remedy for the disease. Crotalus Cascavella is for when the whole body is tense, but the neck most stiff of all. Especially indicated when also there are horrible visions of death. A nice Jewish remedy.

Atoning for His grouchiness one additional remedy at least He sends. This is Rhus Tox. Comes in handy when in sudden need of exodus, relief is gained through ambulation. General activity but especially stretching reduces tension in the neck and generally. Made from the poison ivy botanical Rhus Tox, it also cures itching as in, Oy, am I itching to get the hell out of here!

# Sheygetz
Gentile male, attractive to Jewish women. Best we call him a charming devil

*Lachesis*

We have met the Lachesis *sheygetz* before. The talkative, manipulative type. A seductive **macher.**

# Shikker

Drinker or drunkard

*Odem yesode meofe vesofe leofe, beyno—lveyno iz gut a trink bronfn*
A man comes from the dust and in the dust he will end; and in the meantime it is good to drink vodka


*Acetic Acidum*  *Crotalus Horridus*
*Ethyl Alcohol*  *Lachesis*
*Many of the Lanthanide remedies*

*L'Chaim!*

Acetic Acidum will help the long-time *shikker*, who has grown weak from his drinking habit.

Crotalus Horridus (American rattlesnake) and Lachesis (Brazilian bushmaster snake) are for alcohol addictive personalities.

The Lachesis person is more talkative, whereas the Crotalus Horridus person is more in need of being independent.

Ethyl Alcohol can be used as a remedy to help the *shikker* who is overly convivial even when not drunk.

Remedies made from the Lanthanides, a rare class of elements found in the Periodic Table of Elements are for people whose need to be independent unfortunately includes an addictive tendency.

# Shlak
Crummy and cheap, shoddy, but can also refer to apoplexy. See also, **Shmatta**

| *Arnica* | *Lachesis* |
|---|---|
| *Opium* | *Sepia* |
| *Sulphur* | |

If he is *shlak* in the sense of having had a stroke give Arnica, Lachesis or Opium.

Someone needing Sepia produces a *shlak* effort from general indifference.

The deluded Sulphur person's effort is *shlak* because to him his own work already appears gloriously beautiful.

A word of advice: *Zei nit kain vyzoso*, (Don't be a damned fool) if your handyman's work is *shlak* get rid of him.

# Shleper
Someone who carries along a heavy burden, or drags himself from place to place

*Carbo Vegetabilis*

Having succumbed to a draining illness, she has never entirely recovered. Now, in her exhausted state she is diagnosed with a mitochondrial illness. Getting out of bed is a big *shlep* to her. When despite feeling chilled she still likes to feel a cool breeze, give her Carbo Vegetabilis, made from the burnt out ember of vegetable matter.

# Shlofen

Sleep. See also, **Khlumus** (dreams)

*Klaineh kinder lozen nit shlofen; groisseh kinder lozen nit ruen*
Small children don't let you sleep, big children don't let you rest

*Cocculus Indicus*
*Natrum Muriaticum*


Cocculus Indicus is for inability to sleep due to staying up with an ill loved one. Also useful to overcome jet lag. The person matching up with this remedy is hypersensitive with an overly acute sense of smell; one who readily grows nauseous.

We have encountered the Natrum Muriaticum person before, particularly in **Tsitsa makher**. Due to her heightened sense of responsibility she is likely to replay the events of the day before bedtime when her worries and the lingering effects of entrenched grief will make her sleepless.

# Shpilkes
Nervous energy, restlessness
*Zitsn oyf shpilkes*
Sitting on needles and pins

*Kali Phosphoricum*
*Silica*
*Coffea*

Nervousness from even the slightest excitement can be treated by the remedy Kali Phosphoricum

Another remedy for *shpilkes* of the self-conscious type is Silica. The Silica person's state is given in the famous homeopathic rubric, "Thinks of nothing but pins," indicating a tendency to notice and become overwhelmed by the smallest of details.

She who matches up with Coffea has *shpilkes*. It feels like having had too much caffeine. Restless gestures she makes and unsettled she feels within. Her blood pressure may rise.

# Shpinkele
Freckles
*Az es zenen nito keyn andere mayles, iz a zumer-shprinkele oykh a mayle*
If a girl has no other virtues, even a freckle can be considered one

*Sulphur*

In the event someone you know is kvetching about having *shpinkele*, the remedy Sulphur may help. To tone down the kvetching that is. In regard to ridding the *shpinkele*, maybe not so much can be done.

# Shtarker

In the positive sense a man of strength, a strong, stout fellow. In the negative sense, criminal "muscle," a leg breaker

*Der oks vais nit fun zein gevureh*
The ox does not know it's own strength

*Agaricus*

Like a **shlimazl** I had to go and cheat at *dreidel* (game played with a four-sided spinning top by children during Hanukkah). Now I'm in for it. He's sending over one of his *shtarkers*, a guy who fights with superhuman strength but also in an uncoordinated way. The stimulus-slowing remedy Agaricus would tame the beast. But will he take the remedy soon enough to save me from a beating?

# Shtup es in toches
Stick it in your ass

*Aesculus Hippocastinum*

Fortunately, *Got shikt di refueh far der makeh* (God sends the remedy for the disease). For the sensation as if the rectum is full of sticks, Aesculus Hippocastinum brings relief.

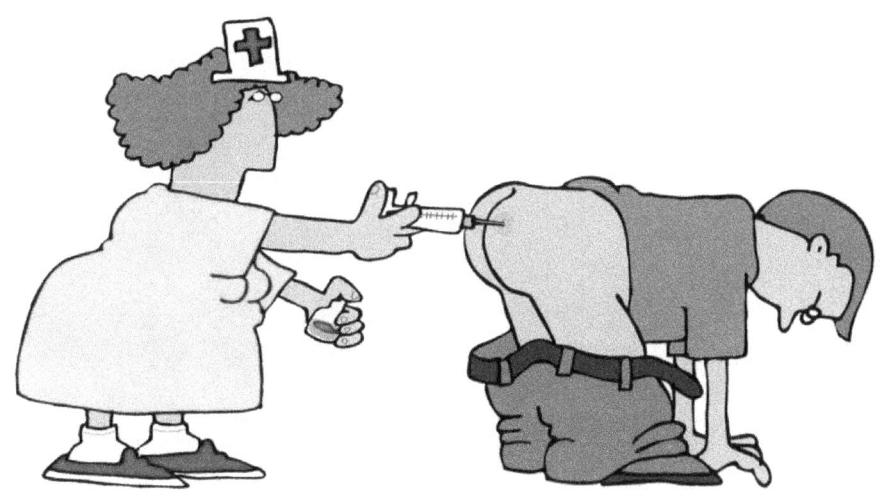

*Go stick it!*

# Shvitzik
Sweaty

*Calcarea Carbonica*  *Mercurius*
*Opium*  *Sepia*
*Lachesis*  *Sulphur*

Many remedy states include unique *shvitzik* features. The following are most prominent:

When *shvitzik* primarily from the head or perspiring all of a sudden, prescribe Calcarea Carbonica.

If she is *shvitzic* all over you give Opium if in addition, she suffers from fright, sleeps deeply and is overall in an escapist mode.

For nightsweats, try Lachesis, Mercurius, Sepia or Sulphur. If you have been reading closely along, by now you should know which and why.

# Tachlis
Pragmatic
*Der shuster ret fun der kopete un der beker ret fun der lopete*
The shoemaker speaks of his last and the baker speaks of his paddle

*Bryonia*
*Natrum Sulphuricum*


What is wrong with having a practical orientation? The answer is that too much of any good thing is a problem. Bryonia comes up for the emotionally dry person who talks and thinks only of business. When injured or sick she is also worse from movement and everywhere dry. Thirsty: not surprising.

Natrum Sulphuricum is a good remedy for someone who even when she has no shortage of **tsores** favors objectivity over kvetching. Apart from that, she is sensitive to mold and usually touchy about being overlooked.

# Treyf
Nonkosher, unclean

*Ammonium Carbonicum*
*Capsicum*
*Psorinum*

He who matches up with Ammonium Carbonicum feels unclean, or has unclean habits. This may come from having a father who has treated him like dirt.

Someone needing Capsicum is unclean because his mucous membranes are dark, red, and spongy; or an oozing, bloody mess. He kvetches of pains that are burning, sore and constricted. He is homesick, nostaligic, weak, lazy, indolent, fat, and lazy. A **batlonim** with unclean habits.

The Psorinum person feels like he has not enough for tomorrow. Also, his skin can look filthy from unhealthiness. Scrubbing has no effect.

# Tzibele
Onion
*Zol ze vaksen ze ve a tzibele mit de kopin dr'erd*
You should grow like an onion with your head in the ground

*Allium Cepa*


A famously perverse *brokh* (curse). The angst motivating its author suggests that she needs a remedy featuring imagination and wretchedness, perhaps Naja (made from cobra venom) On the other hand, were this wondrous directive carried out, how might its recipient feel? Considering onions make you cry, Allium Cepa, a remedy actually made from onion, used to treat burning tears suggests itself. But for crying out loud, could a kvetch of sorrow arise from within the earth?

Underground weeping would be no piece of cake. Alienation and loneliness though, would be on the table. Then, remedies such as Hydrogenium, Camphora and Pulsatilla that silence alienated kvetches can be used. If in Yiddishkeit fashion, the kvetcher feels he's had this punishment coming, then a remedy addressing guilt, meaning a delusion of personal culpability is called for (see, **Shlogen kapores**).

In another scenario the kvetcher defies his own **tsores**, insising, "Hey, my new head suits me just fine and I wouldn't want to be anyplace other than right down here in the dirt!" Such inauthenticity of response and determination to remain stuck suggests Thuja.

# Tsitsa makher
Someone chronically upset and disappointed

*Calcarea Phosphoricum*
*Natrum Muriaticum*
*Phosphoric Acidum*

The Calcarea Phosphoricum individual is a *tsitsa makher* from being the chronic complainer whom bad news upsets out of all proportion. His joints hurt too.

Natrum Muriaticum is for the person who clearly seems sad but won't cry in front of you. *Mazel tov* (good luck) trying to cheer her up. It won't work since she is loyal to her grief. Her subconscious kvetch is: "If I cry I will cry forever. That feels inappropriate so I will not cry, period. I refrain from tears because to overcome a grief as big as this would be a *shanda* (shame), dishonoring the loss." Dispelling this delusion allows tears finally to flow.

Phosphoric Acidum must be given when grief has depleted her. How do we know? Her state of collapse, signaled by lost initiative and indifference is unmistakable.

# Tsores

Trouble, or woes (in the more narrow sense)
*Besser dos besteh fun dem ergsten aider dos ergsteh fun dem besten*
Better the best of the worst than the worst of the best

*Cadmium Muriaticum*              *Nitric Acidum*
*Natrum Muriaticum*               *Psorinum*

If the goal is to express a new-age sentiment such as "You make your own reality," learn a language other than Yiddish. But for blaming or expressing pessimism, you have found your language and lingo. Nevertheless, excessive kvetching merits a remedy:

There is an over-the-top quality to the kvetches emitted by someone needing Cadmium Muriaticum. This remedy is called for in conjunction with mucous membrane dryness, general weakness, and cancerous complaints. Attend closely to his complaints, an underlying theme of thwarted creativity will appear.

Natrum Muriaticum is needed when headaches, nausea and entrenched grief must be contended with.

Nitric Acidum is needed for kvetches that reflect attachment to a grudge. Accompanying symptoms will include mouth sores and gastrointestinal complaints.

Think of Psorinum for someone with lots of **bopkes,** plus itching, despair and obsessive thoughts such as constantly keeping track of what is coming in and going out (a zealous bookkeeper's brain).

## Tsurik shpanung
Back sprain
*Ikh hobn spreynd meyn tsurik*
I sprained my back

*Arnica*
*Sulphur*
*Rhus Tox*

Certainly, as a first recourse give Arnica, the primary remedy for musculo-skeletal trauma.

He needs to be dosed with Sulphur if his mind is also too active and he cannot stand to be overheated.

Rhus Tox should be given if even after *hobn spreynd* his pain is lessened once he has stretched or begun moving around.

## Tumler
Noise maker, agitator. Also means putterer in which case, see **Patshke**

*Cuprum*

People needing Cuprum are loud, vibrant, ambitious and capable of good mimicry. The reason they could use the remedy concerns their *tumling* behavior, itself rooted in inflexibility, with a tendency to develop muscular cramping, and suppressing of emotions (other than anger).

# Tziterdik
Trembling

*Gelsemium*  *Opium*
*Calcarea Carbonicum*  *Staphysagria.*

The Calcarea Carbonica person feels *tziterdik* from thinking he is being observed.

The Gelsemium needing person is *tziterdik* from having had a bad fright or a setback. She will also have a hard time keeping her eyes open and will seek retreat to a quiet room.

Someone needing homeopathic Opium feels an inner trembling from having been frightened, shamed or humiliated. His psyche is in escape mode from reality.

The Staphysagria needing person is innerly *tziterdik* due to fear of an oncoming confrontation.

# Vants

Cockroaches. The term is also applied affectionately to a small child (but then no kvetch is involved)

*Blatta*

This is a good *kllh vort* (curse) to throw at a *farshtinkiner*. But also, if for *vants* on time the exterminator should come! Because with a Yiddish accent "once" sounds just like "vants"; it is maybe only just this *von* time I poke fun. No disrespect intended!

*If just for vants the exterminator should come on time*

Blatta, made from cockroach is actually an important remedy for asthma, especially when it is associated with bronchitis. Why the connection with asthma? *Vants* putrefy food and spread a disgusting odor in the air that harms the lungs.

# Vayb

Wife, or *Balboste*, a competent housewife. Here, oy, we take as our text, lyrics from Morris Rund's *Tsores Fun a Vayb* (Trouble From a Wife) song, whose kvetch is so horrifying only the first stanza is given:

*Ver iz umshtand nokh azoy fil oyshaltn tsores in der shtil*
*A tsore a vaybl hot mir Got bashert giftik iz zi vi a shlang*
*A pisk hot zi vi fayer brent beser volt ikh zi nit derkent*
*Zi iz a klipe arayn zol zi in drerd zi makht mikh shvakh un krank*
*A boarder farglust hot zikh mir in shtib*
*Yetst hert fun mayn vaybl a tayne*
*Zi shrayt nor gevald oy az zi hot im lib*
*Un ikh bin a psule hoshane*
*Koym zog ikh ir: Loz dem boarder geyn!*
*Krig ikh fun ir in tatn arayn*
*un tseshrayt zikh bald af di tseyn!*


Who else has to silently endure such a mess, such troubles?
God chose a real problem wife for me
She's poisonous as a snake.
She's got a mouth on her! It burns like fire.
It would have been better if I'd never met her.
She's a harridan, may she go to hell.
She makes me weak and sick.
I wanted us to have a boarder in the house.
Now I hear my wife's complaint:
She shouts that she loves him
And that I'm as worn out as... limp celery.
As soon as I tell her: let the boarder go!
I really catch it from her.
And she screams through her teeth![11]

---

[11] http://www.yiddishpennysongs.com/2016/03/tsores-fun-vayb-trouble-with-wife-in.html

*Sepia*
*Helonias*


We note that the very sound of the word *vayb* contains *vey*, a lament! But this song goes well beyond the Henny Youngman, "Take my wife…please!" joke. How bitter is the disappointment underlying the *vayb's* lamentations, one must only imagine. It may well be too late, but the remedy Sepia would diminish her anguish.

Not only harridans, but worn out, disappointed *balbostes* will benefit from a dose of Sepia every so often, after feeling too much like an **alter shkrab**.

For the *vayb* utterly exhausted from physical labor, we can also offer Helonias.


# Verem
Worms
*Verem essen toiterhait un deiges lebedikerhait*
Worms eat you up when dead and worries eat you up alive

*Calcarea Carbonica*
*Cina*


The good news is that worms can also eat you up when you are alive. In this situation try Calcarea Carbonica for when the kvetcher fears becoming overwhelmed is the correct remedy.

Cina is called for when the worms cause severe irritation.

## Ver es toig nit far zikh, toig nit far yenem
He who is not good to himself is not good to another

*Saccharum Officinalis*
*Thuja*


The remedy having as its core idea a lack of self-love is Saccharum Officinalis which is discussed more fully in **Cockamamy**.

The self-hating, Thuja state with its **dreykopf** and **moyshe kapoyre** reasoning has also been dealt with, especially, see **Moser**.


## Yentzer
Philanderer. See also, **Sheygetz**
*Zalts im in di oygen, feffer im in di noz*
Throw salt in his eyes, pepper in his nose!

*Fluoric Acidum*


But if she's a *nachshlepper* (head turner) the salt and pepper won't deter him and so give instead Fluoric Acidum.

# Yente

A gossip. Yiddish requires additional words for this behavior and so we have also, *platke makher*

Sholem Aleichem's Yente the Matchmaker is well named, for in brokering a match, knowing everyone else's business confers an advantage.

*The chadchan (broker) heaved a sigh of relief when the man finally broke down and agreed to see the girl she had suggested. It had been a long, tough fight.*

*"There is just one qualification before I accept," the man said, interrupting the broker's happy thoughts. "Before I give my answer I must see her in the nude."*

*"How dare you!" shouted the outraged broker. "What kind of a suggestion is that to make to a nice Jewish girl?"*

*"I insist."*

*The chadchan threw up her hands in resignation, and her reluctance very apparent, went to the girl's house and told her of the fellow's decision. After strenuous objections, indignant tears and refusals she finally agreed to appear before her 'intended' stark naked.*

*"Nu," said the chadchan the next day, "did you find her satisfactory?"*

*"No," said the man. "I didn't like her nose!"*[12]

*Hyoscyamus*
*Culex*


The Hyoscyamus *yente* gossips from being unable to control her silly, shameful and paranoid impulses. Had the candidate bride in the story above, needed this exhibitionistic remedy herself, she would have put up less of a fuss before agreeing to the man's outrageous demand!

---

[12]Adapted from Spalding, H. D. *Encyclopedia of Jewish Humor*. New York, USA: Jonathan David Publishers; 1969; 144.

When the *platke makher* is especially annoying and persistent then it can be she needs Culex, made from mosquito! The company of such a *yente* is like being surrounded by a swarm of hungry mosquitoes, hard to ignore.

# Yerushe
Inheritance
*Hint beissen zikh iber a bain un availim iber a yerusheh*
Dogs fight over a bone and mourners over an inheritance

Also:

*Es ken zein barb, oich di reichsteh arb.*
The richest inheritance can become a burden

*Argentum Metallicum*


Squabbling over an inheritance creates, nebbish, a special kind of stress. This is alleviated by Argentum Metallicum in whose wake the need to garner a legacy becomes less urgent.

# Zaftig
Voluptuous

*Ignatia*  
*Pulsatilla*  
*Calcarea Carbonicum*

*Cocullus Inidicus*  
*Luna*  
*Carcinosin*

*Zaftig aun shpas*  
Voluptuous and fun

Behold, and treasure the gorgeous *zaftig* woman! By virtue of being Venusian, according to Leon Vannier in his book *Typology in Homoeopathy*,[13] she is possessed of a sensual and emotional nature. This means that at one time or another she may need a remedy such as Ignatia, Pulsatilla, Cocullus Indicus, Luna, or Carcinosin. But if she is nonstop kevtching about being overweight, the matter will need rethinking. Calcarea Carbonica can help if the profile fits (cautious, safety- and security-oriented, tending to sweat from the head, and easily overwhelmed) and she gains weight easily.

---

[13]Vannier, L. *Typology in Homoeopathy*. Beaconsfield, Bucks, England: Beaconsfield Publishers, Ltd.; 1992.

# INDEX OF REMEDIES

Acetic Acidum, 139-140
Adamas, 43
Aesculus Hippocastinum, 145
Aethusia Cynapium, 92
Agaricus, 44, 97
Agnus Castus, 135
Allium Cepa, 149
Aloe, 113
Alumina, 45, 53, 62-63, 67
Ammonium Carbonicum 24, 47, 82, 99, 124, 148
Amniotic Fluid, 77
Anacardium, 40, 59, 60, 120, 124
Androctonus, 41
Angustera Vera, 124
Anhalonium, 66
Antimonium Crudum, 60, 80, 96
Antimonium Tartaricum, 47, 64, 122, 126
Apis, 36, 76, 81, 112, 122, 132
Aranea Diadema, 134
Argentum Metallicum, 159
Argentum Nitricum, 36, 115
Arnica, 121, 127, 140, 152
Arsenicum Album, 18, 116, 126
Arum Triphyllum, 107
Asafoetida, 87
Aurum, 70-71, 104, 109, 123
Baryta Carbonica, 54, 86, 94-95, 97, 99
Bismuth, 78
Blatta, 154
Bothrops, 72
Bovista, 99, 115
Bromium, 27
Bryonia, 112
Bufonis, 95
Cadmium Muriaticum, 151
Calcarea Carbonica, 146, 153, 156, 160-161

Calcarea Fluorica, 102-103, 105-106
Calcarea Phosphoricum, 124, 128-130, 150
Calcarea Silicata, 59
Camphora, 61
Cannabis Indicus, 38, 64, 66, 79
Capsicum, 122, 148
Carbo Animalis, 103
Carbo Vegetabilis, 19, 110, 137, 141
Carcinosin, 92, 160-161
Causticum, 34, 92, 136
Cenchris, 35
Chelidonium, 16, 134
China Officinalis, 126
Cicuta Virosa, 39
Cimicifuga, 74
Cina, 117, 156
Cobaltum, 15, 48
Cocculus Indicus, 142
Coffea, 143
Crotalus Cascavella, 34, 138
Crotalus Horridus, 139-140
Culex, 123, 158-159
Cuprum, 76, 114, 122, 152
Cyclamen, 53, 55, 123
Cygnus X-1, 127
Dendroaspis Polyepsis, 35
Digitalis, 34
Drosera, 17
Dulcamera, 16
Elaps, 72
Equisetum, 136
Ethyl Alcohol, 139-140
Fluoric Acidum, 21, 44, 73, 157
Formica, 123
Gadolinium, 40
Gallium Metallicum, 14
Gelsemium, 112, 116
Germanium, 87
Granitum, 25
Graphites, 55

Helleborus, 75, 129
Helonias, 89
Hepar Sulfuris, 106, 112
Hydrocyanicum Acidum, 118-119
Hydrogenium, 149
Hyoscyamus, 21, 45-46, 76, 90, 95, 158
Ignatia, 65, 84, 87, 160-161
Imponderables, 77-78, 177
Iodium, 128
Kali Bichromicum, 52, 81, 92
Kali Bromatum, 48-49
Kali Carbonicum, 57, 86, 100, 120. 137
Kali Phosphoricum, 143
Lac Caninum, 48, 59-60, 74-75
Lac Equinum, 82, 99
Lachesis, 18, 20, 36, 42, 63, 69, 74, 137-140, 146
Lac Humanum, 15
Lac Maternum, 27
Lanthanide remedies, 139-140
Leprominium, 118-119
Lilium Tigranum, 48-49, 68
Lipitorium, 28
Lithium Carbonicum, 88
Luna, 77-78, 80, 160-161
Lycopodium, 37, 40, 54, 68, 96, 98, 107-108, 110, 120, 134, 137
Magnesium Carbonicum, 17
Magnesium Muriaticum, 17
Magnesium Phosphoricum, 122
Mancinella, 23
Mandragora, 23, 136
Medorrhinum, 44, 111
Mercurius, 64, 109, 111, 146
Mezerium, 68
Moschus, 132, 134
Muriatic Acidum, 113
Naja, 63
Natrum Carbonicum, 44
Natrum Muriaticum, 8-11, 116, 142, 150-151
Natrum Sulphuricum, 17, 80, 121, 147
Neodimium Fluorica, 44

Niccolum, 43
Nitric Acidum, 31-33, 53, 86, 130, 152
Nux Moschata, 80
Nux Vomica, 41, 86, 108, 119, 124, 132
Opium and other drug derived remedies, 63, 140, 146, 153
Palladium, 20, 33, 37, 39
Paris Quadrifolia, 20
Petrolium, 65
Phosphoric Acidum, 150
Phosphorus, 45, 77, 92
Platina, 39-40, 86, 104
Plumbum, 97, 114
Podophyllum, 126
Polonium, 103
Psorinum, 60, 87, 105-106, 123, 129, 148, 151
Pulsatilla, 109, 149, 160
Rhododendrum, 80
Rhus Tox, 90, 138, 152
Ruta Graveolens, 17
Saccharum Officinalis, 35, 42, 130, 157
Secale Cornutum, 68-69
Selenium, 135
Sepia, 57, 84, 89, 140, 146, 156
Silica, 14, 64, 112, 143
Solanum Tuberosum Aegrotans, 58-59
Staphysagria, 102, 122, 153
Stramonium, 15, 46-47, 70-71, 76, 97, 134
Sulphur, 19, 28, 43, 50, 62-63, 79, 108-109, 131, 140, 146, 152
Sulphuric Acidum, 53-54
Tarentula Hispanica, 53, 131
Thuja, 33, 52, 84-85, 111, 117, 124, 149, 157
Tuberculinum, 44, 72, 120
Veratrum Album, 26, 42, 46, 69-71, 112
Vipera, 34
Viscum Album, 27
Zincum, 124-125

# APPENDIX

## Finding a Professional Homeopath

Whether it is a garden-variety gripe or a cry from the soul, a homeopath can treat the kvetch. This is because he or she is a generalist, trained to treat just about any condition. Few homeopaths are also psychotherapists and it is not necessary to limit your search to such a hybrid. Rather, you should find a homeopath who is well-trained and with whom you feel comfortable, since you will be disclosing personal information. A professional homeopath is someone who uses homeopathy as their only (or primary) modality, not someone who uses it for minor symptom relief while addressing your health condition with another practice like acupuncture or chiropractic.

A professional homeopath may or may not have a license in another health care modality (except in the US, in a small number of states requiring them to be MDs).

Many homeopaths started out as medical doctors, nurse practitioners, pharmacists, chiropractors, or acupuncturists who wanted to add the power of homeopathy to the modalities they offer their clients. Others headed directly to professional homeopathy training without going through conventional medical training first. Either way, ideally they will have the CCH credential (Certified Classical Homeopath, indicating the person is nationally certified after 1000 hours of training).

Check www.HomeopathicDirectory.org. However, there are good homeopaths who do not have this credential, sometimes because they were already in practice when the credential was created 20 years ago, sometimes because their practice is so busy they don't feel the need for the credential. This is especially true of MD homeopaths. They are rare and you are lucky if you can find one.

As of now there are only about 500 CCH-certified homeopaths in the United States, so you may need to use word of mouth. Ask at your local health food store, or ask another holistic practitioner (such as your chiropractor, acupuncturist or massage therapist) if they know of a good homeopath.

You can also consult the directory of the National Center for Homeopathy: www.nationalcenterforhomeopathy.org, look under Resources. Please note though, that anyone can list herself or himself in this directory. The NCH does not evaluate credentials, although it lists whatever credentials the homeopath has.

Council for Homeopathic Certification
http://www.homeopathicdirectory.com/
North American Society of Homeopaths
http://www.homeopathy.org/ National Center for Homeopathy
http://nationalcenterforhomeopathy.org/

Other Right Whale Press books you may like are available at www.rightwhalepress.com or Amazon.com

*"Medicine and illness cure one another. The whole earth is medicine. Where do you find the self?"*

# —Master Unmon
# Acclaim for Interpreting Chronic Illness

The first, genuinely integrative medicine text.
Psychologists and psychotherapists may delve into the clinical possibilities raised by the book's self-diagnosis mandala and the startling capability it offers of interpreting multifactorial symptoms. Physicians, nurses, alternative practitioners, or chiropractors investigating integrative medicine will welcome Interpreting Chronic Illness for its clinical relevance: the physician may look to broaden the concepts of health and healing; the homeopath will appreciate its fresh materia medica; the practitioner of Traditional Chinese Medicine will value how the book's updating of the Five Phases heightens the ancient system's relevance.

Jerry Kantor has successfully integrated the disciplines of homeopathy, Traditional Chinese Medicine, and biomedicine into pragmatic healing approaches that busy practitioners can readily and easily apply to common clinical presentations. Multimodal management and integrative medicine techniques, while certainly the best approach to medical conditions, can be deceptively complex. Jerry's explanations and guidelines are the perfect balance of background information and recommendations allowing the clinician to effectively supplement their treatment armamentarium.

—Mark Scheutzow MD, PhD, DHom, NMD, FAAIM, DABHM, DAAPM

I know of no other body of work, in the science of homeopathic medicine, which demystifies the core essence of homeopathic Materia Medica as does Kantor's brilliant work. A truly integrative, evidence-based perspective that should be mandatory reading for all practitioners of the art, science and philosophy of homeopathy.

—Georgianna Donadio, PhD Florence Nightingale Scholar and Director of the National Institute of Whole Health

A brilliant and groundbreaking work by an integrative practitioner who 'speaks the language' of three very different healing paradigms–biomedicine (modern Western medicine), Traditional Chinese Medicine and homeopathy. By illumining each in the light of the others, he brings the CAM modalities from a subservient role as 'alternative medicine' to full participation as Five Elements model of acupuncture; provides fresh insights into the major homeopathic remedies based on the Five Elements model; and shows how both can address the diagnostic categories of biomedicine. This will be an essential book for practitioners and students of all three modalities who want to expand their healing paradigm.

—Begabati Leninhan, RN, CCH, Former Director of the Teleosis School of Homeopathy

This book is a major triangulation of multi-medical perspectives that add to our understanding of what healing is about. Jerry Kantor has done a great job!

—Ted Kaptchuk, OMD author, *The Web That Has No Weaver: Understanding Chinese Medicine*

A seminal work of probing, integrative intelligence, Jerry Kantor's Interpreting Chronic Illness systematically lays out how Nature, personal temperament and life experience constitute the crucible for chronic illness and, in turn, the laboratory for self-understanding. It will consolidate and advance the thinking of practitioners of acupuncture and homeopathy, and will challenge Western-trained health care professionals to think of illness and disease as more than just invading pathogens.

—Eugene L. Pogany, Ph.D., Clinical Psychologist, author of In My Brother's Image

Much of American medicine is based on the belief that disease is an entity that flies through the air and lands on the unlucky, whereupon we 'do battle' with it. Jerry Kantor persuades us otherwise with his thoroughly original coalescence of the best of Eastern and Western views of diagnosis and treatment. I won't let another physician touch me until he/she has read this book.

—William Martin Sloane, Ph.D., Vice President American Association of Integrative Medicine


This is an excellent book for those of us who would like to use both Traditional Chinese Medicine including Acupuncture and Homeopathy to treat patients.

—Zhaoming Chen, MD, PhD, MS, CFP, FAAIM Chair and Chief Spokesman, American Association of Integrative Medicine Diplomate of Neurology and Clinical Neurophysiology, American Board of Psychiatry and Neurology Licensed Acupuncturist Certified Qigong Instructor Tai Chi Master .


Jerry Kantor has produced a book that is wise, perceptive, practical and immediately applicable, but that will also yield further riches on deep study. It draws on the three apparently incompatible fields of acupuncture, homeopathy and modern biomedicine, and weaves from them whole cloth: a patterned approach to understanding chronic illness, and guidelines for treatment. Worthy of serious consideration.

—Steven Clavey, BA Dip Adv Acupuncture, author of *Fluid Physiology and Pathology in Chinese Medicine*

# Acclaim for The Toxic Relationship Cure

Using engaging and memorable vignettes, The Toxic Relationship Curediscusses how homeopathy is used constitutionally for clients suffering mental,
emotional and physical damage consequent to prolonged toxic and unhealthy life relationships. The book fills a vacuum in the homeopathic library where despite the presence of numerous, excellent self-help and acute prescribing texts little exists to help the layperson understand homeopathy's relevance to longstanding maladies rooted in psychic or spiritual crisis.

—Loretta Butehorn PhD, CCH


It is always a special pleasure to have a book exceed even my highest expectations, and this book did. Jerry Kantor's The Toxic Relationship Cure is crammed with practical insights into seventy-two homeopathic medicines and their body/mind typology. Using vivid, composite case histories Kantor illuminates specific homeopathic medicines with an eye to how each can reflect the impact of a
problematic relationship. Kantor's book goes several steps further than most other homeopathic texts by venturing to describe a needed homeopathic remedy's medical and psychological impact. Further, his description of both well-known
and little-known remedies offers valuable differentiation among remedies similar to the remedy under discussion.

—Dana Ullman, MPH
Homeopathic Educational Services

# Also by Jerry Kantor, available at Amazon.com

# A review from Helios Homeopathy

This is an extremely comprehensive account of some of the many different approaches to helping with autism. Marrying traditional Chinese medicine, with its accent on healthy organ-function – to other therapeutics, the author presents a Smorgasbord of treatments.

Of these, the homeopathic approach, as pioneered by Tinus Smits, with his CEASE therapy, is central. The author, himself trained in the CEASE method, describes how it works by helping detoxify a system overloaded by, for example, heavy metals, antibiotics, pesticides, and vaccinations.

As well as considering some obvious physiological problems such as leaky gut, there is a marked emphasis on the esoteric. Protocols are described, but it is emphasized that there is no routine way of undoing the havoc of ASD (Autistic Spectrum Disorder).

The practitioner must be alert to all sorts of influences on which a prescription may be based—including the mother's emotional and physical state in pregnancy, ongoing dysfunction within the family, environmental triggers, miasmatic heritage, and so on. A flexible and creative approach is therefore required by the practitioner.
This methodology is described as "The Sine Wave Method" in which prescribing between drainage/ constitutional/ and further drainage and detox, is likened to the motion of a wave.

Along the way, many other unusual treatment modalities are touched upon, including the Unda numbers, (which assist, a bit like Tissue Salts in detox, but are a lot more complex than these); Meditatively Proved remedies, and a number of "Matridonal Remedies" such as Placenta, Vernix and the Lac's.

A number of cases are given to illustrate the approach, and many resources, web sites, etc., are included in the appendices. If you are treating ASD children, then this will prove an invaluable Desktop Reference.